SECRET CONTENDERS:

The Myth of Cold War Counterintelligence

SECRET
By
MELVIN BECK

CONTENDERS

The Myth of Cold War Counterintelligence

Introduction By Thomas Powers

 SHERIDAN SQUARE PUBLICATIONS, INC.

New York, New York

Note: This book represents another in a series of in-depth studies of current intelligence issues. For details, write to Sheridan Square Publications, Inc., P. O. Box 677, New York, NY 10013.

ISBN: Hardbound: 0-940380-05-6

Paperback: 0-940380-04-8

Library of Congress Cataloging in Publication Data:

Beck, Melvin, 1913-
 Secret contenders.

 Includes index.
 1. Beck, Melvin, 1913-   . 2. Intelligence agents—
United States—Biography. 3. United States. Central
Intelligence Agency—History. 4. World politics—
1945-   . I. Title.
UB271.U52B43 1984   327.1'2'0924 [B] 84-10635
ISBN 0-940380-05-6
ISBN 0-940380-04-8 (pbk.)

Publisher's Note

The author's manuscript was cleared by the Central Intelligence Agency in December 1975, while the Agency was under investigation by the Church Committee. After several years, when we expressed our interest in publication to the author, we learned that the author had revised and expanded the original draft, though leaving required deletions intact. In the present climate of ambiguity about the legal status of the reclassification of information, both author and publisher decided to proceed with the original, cleared draft. It contained relatively few deletions, all of which are noted herein. The manuscript was edited only for style, order, consistency, and the like. Any and all differences between this publication and the cleared manuscript are due to our editors, not to the author.

Dedication

This book is dedicated to Americans who believe in and uphold the principles upon which the United States was founded, including the free flow of ideas.

Acknowledgments

I wish to acknowledge the support and understanding of my wife, Judith, and of our son, Laurence, and our daughter, Janis, during my prolonged intelligence career. My thanks go to Thomas Powers, author of "The Man Who Kept the Secrets," whose critique of my manuscript lent solidity to my examination of clandestine intelligence. I acknowledge, too, the conscientiousness and fairmindedness of editors Ellen Ray and William Schaap, who guided the book to publication.

Table of Contents

Preface

THIS book is about the Clandestine Services of the Central Intelligence Agency. Its focus is on my eight years as an operations case officer of the Soviet division, spearhead of the Cold War contest between the CIA and the Soviet KGB.

It is necessary to clarify at the outset that I attempt no sweeping appraisal of the CIA, pro or con. It should be understood that the Clandestine Services functions officially only as an appendage to the main part of the Agency which carries out the centralized tasks for which the CIA was formed. In discharging these tasks more in keeping with its charter, the Agency provides the personnel, tools and procedures by which research and analysis are performed to result in finished and evaluated intelligence. For some perverse reason, performance of outstanding services by the non-clandestine components of the CIA has been publicly overlooked: Analysts are undifferentiated in the public eye from their covert colleagues.

Taken at large, the Central Intelligence Agency, including the Clandestine Services, is a professional organization dedicated to performing its job honorably and well. In its zeal, however, the Clandestine Services often strayed into activities that were not its job or in its charter, and these errant journeys were made, not by the CIA as an organization, but at the urging of shortsighted, irrational people in power who defied reform and retained their ideological blinders throughout the Agency's history. These same centers of entrenched power were responsible for implanting an unreasoning Cold War attitude and almost fanatical anti-communist stance that undermined the purposes for which the Agency was created.

Introduction

MELVIN Beck spent 27 years in the intelligence business, the first ten mainly as a Soviet analyst with the National Security Agency, and the rest — from 1953 until his retirement in 1971 — with the Central Intelligence Agency. A heart condition restricted him to a desk in Washington until late 1958 when a chance encounter at an office Christmas party got him a job as chief of the Latin American desk in the Soviet division of the Clandestine Services. Latin America was no plum in 1958, but luck intervened. Fidel Castro came to power at the turn of the year and the CIA immediately scrambled to determine what his relationship would be to the Soviet Union. For the next eight years Beck spent most of his time as a case officer in Cuba and Mexico running operations against the Soviets in the field. In Cuba he mainly worked as an "inside" man — a regular member of the Havana station under light State Department cover. Later, in Mexico, he was an "outside" man — meaning that he was ostensibly a private citizen and had no overt contact with the CIA station attached to the U.S. Embassy.

Beck's book demonstrates that CIA operations against the Soviets were carried out within a counterintelligence framework, converting them to double agent operations whenever possible. Their overriding purpose was to penetrate the defenses of the KGB or GRU in order to divine what the Soviets were secretly interested in. The Russian Intelligence Service had the same mission, and it was the ensuing contest that characterized Cold War counterintelligence.

What did all this clandestine scurrying to and fro amount to in the larger scheme of the Cold War? In Beck's view, very little. Experience in the field taught him that the "secret war" in counterintelligence was largely a charade. American and Soviet case officers, the secret contenders, ran few risks. When operations failed it was the agents who suffered. Spy fiction, Beck found, is just that. There is no gun play in the real world, no midnight car chases through rain-swept streets, just the quiet meetings of nondescript men in bars and public parks, followed by the tedious writing of reports. Beck found that most operational activity was conducted for its own sake, in order to look busy for the bosses back at Headquarters.

More importantly, Beck concludes that propaganda operations have little impact on uncontrolled foreign audiences; the real target of operations in the field was opinion at home. This is a subtle point, but a significant one; I have never seen it argued so clearly elsewhere.

Beck's career in the field was full of the unexpected. In one story, he describes at length his role in a scientific experiment which promised an almost Copernican revolution in the area of tradecraft. This was a peculiarly American undertaking. Intelligence agencies tend to reflect their national origin. The Poles, it is said, are romantic and daring, or at least used to be; the British sophisticated but poor, the French cynical, the Germans methodical, the Russians crude, thorough and relentless. The Americans, heir to a long tradition of Yankee tinkering, have a weakness for the quick technological fix, the "magic bullet" which will cut through all difficulties. During the 1950s and '60s, for example, the CIA experimented with a host of drugs intended to solve problems endemic in the intelligence business. One pill was intended to induce a selective amnesia in agents retiring from the field. The idea was to wipe the mental slate clean of all operational detail, so the spy-runners could sleep at night without worrying that disgruntled former operatives were being plied with drinks by the gentlemen in shiny Polish suits from the Committee for State Security of the Union of Soviet Socialist Republics or — worse yet! — American journalists. Such a drug is a pharmacological fantasy; the human brain does not collect operational detail in a convenient corner where it might be blotted up without sweeping away memory of the agent's wife and kids as well.

You can see the possibilities here, with just about any "person of interest" to the CIA — a KGB officer, perhaps, or a Cuban diplomat, a member of the Egyptian Communist Party, a Soviet physicist visiting the West on a scientific exchange, the Saudi Arabian oil minister, the chief operating officer of the Bank for International Settlements. He might be programmed to spill the beans on a continuing basis. The secrets held by such persons do not simply fall into a "nice to know" category. They are the very heart and essence of what it is that intelligence agencies try to find out.

In Beck's encounter with a double agent of doubtful loyalty, the idea was to use a new technique of instant hypnosis to establish once and for all whether the agent was really working for the Russians, or for the Americans as he claimed. This is always a difficult problem. A former counterintelligence officer once told me that his last job for the Agency before retirement was a special study of double agent or DA operations. I asked how the study turned out; were they working for us or them? "Well," he said, with a shrug of inexpressible weariness, "it's impossible to say. That's why I did the study." It was the purpose of instant hypnosis to end these troubling doubts; with Beck's double agent, instant hypnosis might have been to the history of intelligence what gunpowder was to the history of warfare.

The bizarre experiment, as Beck describes it, was a hilarious failure; but it and other double agent and counterintelligence stories in Beck's interesting book touch upon many of the major themes of the history of American clandestine intelligence since the founding of the CIA in 1947. Foremost, of course, is the fascination with the shortcut, the search for a technical means to bypass all the subtle arts of agent recruitment and management so that intelligence of the most important sort — the things that only *people* know — might be scooped up on an industrial scale. Equally typical was the failure.

The CIA was not founded in reaction to the onset of the Cold War, as often supposed, but in the wake of a congressional investigation of the surprise attack on Pearl Harbor, conducted at the end of the Second World War. Among the conclusions of this study was a finding that ample warning of the attack had been available, but only in bits and pieces strewn about Washington. An example frequently cited was the white smoke which poured in thick clouds from the Japanese Embassy in Washington shortly before the outbreak of war — an unmistakable sign the Japanese were burning their diplomatic files. This sort of thing ought to sound alarm bells. Another potentially important piece of evidence was the disappearance of the Japanese fleet, meaning it had imposed radio silence. The problem in December 1941 was that no one was explicitly assigned to gather intelligence of this kind in a central place so that the pieces might be fitted together into a revealing whole. Hence the Central Intelligence Agency, initially intended to be an all-source repository and analytical shop which would produce "finished intelligence," or "paper" as it is commonly called.

But government agencies share with cancer a built-in desire to *grow*. Almost immediately the CIA began to expand its writ and inflate its mandate. It quickly absorbed some odd limbs from the Office of Strategic Services, closed down by President Truman at the end of World War II. Principal among these was the old X-2 counterintelligence division of the OSS, which had been parked in the War Department for a couple of years, along with the SI or "secret intelligence" branch. This put the CIA in the spy-running business. In 1948 the White House, alarmed by the prospect of a Communist victory in the Italian elections scheduled for that year, created a new organization to conduct clandestine operations. Eventually called the Office of Policy Coordination (OPC), its first job was to encourage a victory by the Christian Democrats in Italy, which it did. The OPC was not at first a component of the CIA exactly, although it was formally placed under the authority of the Director of Central Intelligence. (In 1952 it was merged with the CIA's espionage branch, the Office of Special Operations, and renamed the Deputy Directorate for Plans.) Thus by the end of 1948 the structure and preoccupations of the CIA had already assumed the form they still take today. Espionage, counterintelligence, and covert action operations were part of the Agency's job, with pride of place going to the latter throughout most of the CIA's history; the target was the Russians (and their surrogates in the form of local Communist Parties), and the arena was the world.

It is a truism of the intelligence business that its job is to plumb an enemy's "capabilities and intentions." This may sound straightforward enough but as a practical matter the two are very different. "Capabilities" — that is, an enemy's armed forces — are neutral (we claim our own military is purely defensive in purpose, for example, and therefore need be a cause for worry to none), while "intentions" — what an enemy plans to do — may not be known even to himself. Capabilities are concrete; they are things like tanks, divisions, capital ships, or strategic missiles. They are knowable in the same way that the geography of a mountain range is knowable, and they are almost as hard to hide.

The CIA, along with other intelligence agencies, is best at three jobs — finding things, counting things, and describing things. The KGB and the GRU, the two principal Russian intelligence agencies, are good at these things too. When Truman told Stalin about the atomic bomb during a meeting in Potsdam in July 1945, for example, Stalin already knew all about it from the reports of Russian spies who had been privy to the Manhattan Project's work at Los Alamos. In the four decades of strategic weapons development since 1945 there have been no major surprises on either side. The history of

American intelligence is full of inter-agency acrimony about what the Russians were building at any given moment — the "missile gap" is only the best known of the wild surmises sometimes made in Washington — but the arguments were always settled long before the weapons were actually in place and thus posed a potential threat. The Russians must have had their arguments about the "out years" as well, but the available evidence suggests that they, too, pretty generally knew what we were up to before actual deployments which really mattered. The beginning of reconnaissance flights over the Soviet Union by high-altitude U-2 spy planes in 1956 dispelled most of the uncertainty about Soviet weapons programs, and the advent of satellite photography in 1960 solved the problem once and for all. The plain fact is that no important weapons system is small enough to hide successfully. Thus it may be taken as a given that both sides have a good grasp of the other's capability — what it has actually *got* in the way of weaponry.

That leaves "intentions," a far more elusive quarry. What is an intention anyway? The minutes of a secret meeting of the Politburo? The personal agenda of the President of the U.S. or the General Secretary of the Communist Party of the Soviet Union? How do you recognize it when you see it? An intention is not a concrete thing like a tank park, a nuclear weapons storage depot, or a phased-array radar — something which can be located and photographed. An intention is a state of mind. Grandiose intentions like a desire for world dominion may be doubted to exist in any real way at all. They fall into the realm of pious hopes. American and Soviet leaders, like politicians everywhere, routinely pay lip service to pious hopes. On national holidays there is much windy talk of "the success of freedom" and the "triumph of world socialism." An intention is just gossamer until it narrows down to something a government or official *can* do — make a speech, grant a loan, sign a treaty, dispatch a fleet, or, conceivably, fire one or more nuclear weapons. A significant intention can be written down on a piece of paper, distributed in a limited number of copies, and locked up in a safe at night. This makes it hard to get at. During World War II the British cipher experts at Bletchley Park learned to read German radio traffic, which told them, among other useful things, what the Germans planned to do. Forewarned is forearmed. This ability probably had more to do with Churchill's confidence and determination in the dark years of 1940-41 than any other single factor.

But tactical intentions are one thing, strategic intentions quite another. In peacetime the latter tend to loom large, and may become objects of obsessive argument. Before World War I the British spent years arguing about the German naval building program. Was it intended to challenge Britain's supremacy over the seas? Or was it only the natural expression of a growing power newly conscious of its own strength? The Americans, after all, were building a big navy too, but it did not alarm Whitehall to a similar degree. Since 1945 the inner circles of the American government have been arguing about Soviet strategic intentions. Why did Stalin retain his huge land army in the late 1940s while the Americans dismantled theirs in such a hurry that General George C. Marshall likened it to "a rout"? Why did Stalin impose client regimes in Eastern Europe? Was the challenge posed by the Communist Parties of France and Italy evidence that Stalin intended to bring all Europe under Russian hegemony? Was the North Korean invasion of South Korea in June 1950 encouraged by Russia as a deliberate test of American will? Or were these things all the natural responses of a frightened government to the threat implicit in American monopoly (until 1949) of atomic weapons, and the fact that U.S. production of fissionable materials did not skip a beat with the ending of the war?

Historians of the Cold War are still trying to sort out the tangled matrix of cause and effect, but even within American intelligence agencies the argument was heated. One group insisted that Russian policy was animated by a larger purpose which amounted to a plan to conquer, or at least dominate, the world. A second group, generally on the defensive, argued that security was the real aim of Soviet policy. Behind this debate, which continues today, lies a rarely examined question:

Can a nation have an "intention" in the broad sense of the word? Or is its behavior determined by history, geography and national character? The CIA's Board of National Estimates wrestled with this question every year while writing its Annual Survey of Soviet Intentions and Capabilities, a piece of intelligence paper which grew from perhaps 25 pages in the late 1940s to multiple volumes with appendices filled with reams of supporting data. One early chairman of the BNE, William Langer, said, "Our answer [to the question of intentions] is to say nothing is going to happen in the forseeable future, and say it in the most alarming way possible." In 1975 George Bush, then Director of Central Intelligence, brought in a team of outside experts to go over the national estimate. Working with the same evidence used by the CIA's Soviet analysts, the "B Team" came up with a sharply different, much more alarmist view of Soviet intentions. What this exercise mainly proved was that intentions are in the eye of the beholder.

As Beck shows, American intelligence agencies, constantly pressed by policy makers who want simple answers to the big questions, do not know what is going on inside the Soviet government, and despite enormous efforts, never have known. What the Soviets say publicly is predictable or opaque, and what they do is ambiguous. Russian secrecy is nothing new. The Bolsheviks and their predecessors were schooled in secrecy during the decades of underground struggle with the Czarist regime before the revolution in 1917. After the revolution the Communist Party felt threatened and tried to hide its weakness. The extraordinary breadth of Stalin's personal power for nearly 30 years, and his arbitrary use of it to kill his enemies during the purges of the 1930s, only confirmed the tendency toward secrecy. The centralization of power is another old tradition in Russia, and secrecy goes hand in hand with a monopoly on power. All political leaders try to hide the gap between what they say and what they really think, but Soviet leaders are better at it than most. The result is that very little is known in the West about Russian political leaders. When Yuri Andropov came to power following the death of Leonid Brezhnev in December 1982, early reports described him as a liberal, a fan of Western jazz and popular novels, and an avid tennis player. This was all purest fantasy. It was soon apparent that Andropov could barely walk unaided; if he had ever played tennis — and there are few courts in Moscow — those days were long behind him.* After Andropov's death in February 1984, Western journalists were startled to learn that his wife, Tatyana, was still alive.

But it was not only the press which was in the dark about Andropov's character, his personal history, and his intentions. Intelligence agencies were in the same boat. The Soviet Politburo rules one of the world's two great powers, but its politics are a closed book. How these dozen men look at the world, the degree to which they represent domestic constituencies like the military or agriculture; what they read and think; how they view the West; their relations with each other; what they hope for their country — all are hidden. Even a relatively straightforward question about something as elementary as the Soviet motives for deploying SS-20 intermediate-range missiles pointed at Europe cannot be answered with confidence. The Soviets insist this was a modernization program pure and simple, but one may doubt. The SS-20s are accurate; they are solid-fuelled and thus quick to fire; each carries three independently targetable warheads, or MIRVs; and they can hit anything from the Urals to the Atlantic. Anyone facing nearly 1000 SS-20 warheads, as the Europeans do, is bound to take note. Were the Soviets trying to intimidate and "Finlandize" Western Europe, as some intelligence analysts claim? It's anybody's guess. The Russians won't say.

It is a rule of thumb in the intelligence business that operations are difficult to conduct from inside a target country, as was the case with Beck's mission in Cuba and, for example, early CIA cross-border operations in the Soviet Union. In the 1920s and '30s, for example, Western intelligence services

---

*When the Italian spy Bruno Pontecorvo, a physicist, moved to Moscow, he discovered to his amazement that his run-of-the-mill game made him one of the city's top players.

watched the Russians from large stations maintained in Riga on the Baltic coast. More recently Berlin has offered a similar door to the East. The Russians appear to share this theory. The FBI has long insisted that its hands are full watching Soviet diplomats, many suspected of being KGB officers, based in the United States, but the Bureau is probably exaggerating the problem. Soviet diplomats attached to the embassy in Washington and their mission to the United Nations in New York, for example, all live in suburban compounds. They arrive and depart *en masse* by bus every day, which hardly provides much opportunity for the restless wanderings of case officers trying to service agents. Mexico offers an easier field, and the Soviets have maintained a large embassy there for decades. Indeed it is widely believed in American intelligence circles that the Mexican government tolerates this state of affairs as part of an explicit *quid pro quo* negotiated in the 1920s: no troublesome Mexican Communist Party, in return for granting the Soviets a relatively free hand in conducting intelligence operations targeted on the United States.

Throughout his career in the field Beck ran a wide range of operations, from attempts to bug the apartments and offices of Soviet diplomats and intelligence operatives, to routine servicing of agents — that is, individuals with access to information "of interest" to the CIA. Beck's major preoccupation in Mexico was the running of double agent operations, dealing with people also working simultaneously for the Soviets. The purpose behind DA operations was to gather information about Soviet intelligence officers and their working methods, and to divine what the Soviets were really after by "reading back" from the sort of questions they asked their agents. This is a routine method of intelligence agencies, for whom indirection is a way of life. Sometimes it works brilliantly, as it did for the British in Operation Double-Cross during World War II. Early in the war the British gained control of all German agent networks operating in Britain, which gave them unique access to German thinking and, later, provided an invaluable channel to feed misleading information to the Germans about the date and place of the invasion of Europe. The CIA hopes to reproduce this success with its DA operations targeted on the Russians, but in Beck's case it never amounted to much more than a kind of busy work, "operations for operations' sake," a restless probing of the opposition intended to satisfy the tireless demand for results from CIA headquarters in Langley, Virginia.

All this activity — Beck describes or alludes to several dozen operations — had one overriding purpose: to penetrate Soviet secrecy with agents or technical devices which might allow the CIA to chart the vast unknown sea of Soviet intentions — what they were *really* after. This is not a crazy thing to do, just a hard one. The CIA has not always failed in its efforts; occasionally it has obtained the services of a spy of real value. The best known, Colonel Oleg Penkovskiy, is said to have provided as many as 10,000 pages of documentary material on microfilm, including operational manuals for the SS-4 and SS-5 missiles which Khrushchev tried to spirit into Cuba in 1962. These manuals are said to have allowed the CIA to monitor installation of the missiles on a day-by-day, step-by-step basis, once U-2 photographs had established their presence, with the result that Kennedy *knew* he had time to put political pressure on Khrushchev to remove the missiles before they would be ready to fire. Since Kennedy's advisers had initially been in favor of a preemptive bombing raid on the missile sites, this extra leeway — a classic example of the utility of intelligence — may well have saved the world from war. But Penkovskiy, who was in any event recruited and run by the British, was the exception, not the rule. Beck's experience was more typical. The Soviets he targeted in Cuba and Mexico surrendered little of real significance. Beck's operations were simply episodes in the Great Game.

Finally, Beck makes this point about Cold War intelligence, that the contending intelligence agencies reflect the ideological contest between the United States and the Soviet Union. He gradually came to believe that the Russians conducted an "aggressive" foreign policy in order to look like a great power to their own citizens. They weren't trying to undermine the will of the West, but rather to create an echo abroad of the propaganda themes sounded at home. The Americans, in Beck's view, were doing much the same thing for much the same reasons. Beck says that in effect the legitimacy of rulers on both sides is largely based on their claims as defending champions in a great worldwide struggle. The Soviets present themselves as the bulwark of world socialism, the Americans as defenders of freedom. Without an actual struggle — real conflict in real places — how could rulers justify their vast defense budgets, or their own indispensability? Beck's experience convinced him that operational activity was not directed at any real threat, but only to support the illusion of a threat. This is not an idea likely to win many adherents in either Moscow or Washington, where "the struggle" is a way of life and a *raison d'etre*. The drum-beaters on both sides will dismiss Beck as a tired cynic, and cite chapter and verse about the terrible things the other side is doing in Afghanistan or El Salvador.

Is Beck right? This is hard to say. His theory makes sense of much which is otherwise inexplicable, and it is supported by the average citizen's gut feeling there is something crazy and willful about all this global meddling. Can the average Russian really believe that the fate of Afghanistan has anything to do with *him*? Do ordinary Americans feel genuine alarm that left-wing Salvadoran peasants may soon run all the coffee plantations? These are the sorts of things governments worry about, not people. But even if "the struggle" is not really about anything — has no compelling inner necessity — it is a struggle all the same, and real people get really killed in it. Cuba may matter first and foremost to the Cubans, but it counts for plenty in Moscow and Washington too. The two sides came close to war over Cuba in 1962 and they may do so again.

For the moment the arena of conflict has shifted to Central America, where too many people struggle for life in too small a place with too few resources. If ordinary people ever needed help and sympathy, and above all to be *let alone*, it is there, but that is not what they get. What they get is war on a scale which can be sustained only by great powers with a global strategy in mind, and the money and firepower to back it up. This is El Salvador's tragedy, as it was Vietnam's or Poland's. Nicaragua supports the Salvadoran rebels. Cuba supports Nicaragua. Russia supports Cuba. The United States opposes all of the above with money and weapons and all of the black arts at the CIA's command. Melvin Beck may say all this is crazy, that nothing is at stake to justify Washington's obsession, that it is ordinary people who will suffer whoever wins, and we may agree with him. Indeed I hope it's clear I do agree with him. Who can imagine that anything good will come out of this awful war? Washington "won" in Guatemala in 1954, and the result has been a political nightmare ever since. Can Washington's allies in El Salvador promise anything better? If the rebels win they will inherit an impoverished state obsessed with security, facing the implacable hostility of the colossus to the north.

Cold War is Beck's specialty — the secret probing and testing and maneuvering for advantage by East and West in other people's countries. As Beck describes the struggle in his book, one of the most revealing of the few on an arcane subject, the whole enterprise looks silly, expensive and futile. But Beck does not make the mistake of dismissing such conflicts lightly. El Salvador is what happens when the Cold War gets out of hand.

Thomas Powers
February 1984

1

OPERATIONS OFFICER:
The Road to Havana

IF I had any apprehension about my first spy mission, it was dispelled the moment the plane from Miami hovered over Havana's José Marti International Airport in the early dusk of mid-October 1959, while the lights of the city were blinking a friendly invitation. A Cuban combo, in gaudy costume, greeted the disembarking passengers with a flourish of catchy Latin rhythms. My tourist card and my Brownie camera caused no raised eyebrows, and I was on my way to the Hotel Vedado in the downtown section of Havana, within walking distance of the American Embassy.

Only a year before, after six years as an analyst in the Soviet division of the Clandestine Services*, I was champing to get an operational desk assignment as a stepping stone to an overseas assignment. By chance, at the office Christmas party of 1958, a friend of mine, a colleague of analyst days who had made it to case officer, decidedly in his cups, had asked me whether I wanted to take over the Latin American desk, which was being vacated by a case officer who had wangled an overseas slot in Mexico. I struck like a hungry bass. I gulped my drink and said, "It's a deal." I prevailed on my friend to take me to the chief, who had socked away plenty by this time but who listened politely to the proposition. "Sure," he said, "good idea," and amiably turned back to the festivities. That was it. No bucking, no trading, no dealing. I was so elated I

---

*The term used in the CIA to denote the directorate responsible for clandestine intelligence collection, counterintelligence, and covert operations.

1

gave no thought to the probability that the assignment hardly merited the customary administrative scramble.

Nobody in the Soviet division cared very much about Latin America — paid it much attention, or considered it of any importance whatsoever to the mission of the division. But since the Soviet division had the responsibility of operating against Soviets wherever they might be on the face of the earth, Latin America was necessarily included. My good luck at the Christmas party was that no one knew that a few days later Fidel Castro and his rebel guerrilla army would be making their triumphant entry into Havana.

My first few months of 1959 on the Latin American desk were a blend of area study, language learning, and a slow ingestion of the "feel" for operations. I covered the countries included within the jurisdiction of the so-called "host" division for the area, the Western Hemisphere division. At the time there were only three countries of Latin America that had diplomatic relations with the Soviet Union: Mexico, Argentina, and Uruguay. A few others had unofficial or semi-official relations with the Soviets, mainly with respect to trade. The portents of Castro's assumption of power in Cuba had not been manifested this early, and in the eyes of the Soviet division Latin America still represented little more than the stereotype of a peasant stretched out at the foot of a cactus, a huge sombrero covering his droopy eyes. As for the American public, Castro's earlier "Robin Hood" image still lingered. Perhaps because of the cram course to educate myself about my new area of responsibility, the little I read then about Cuba disposed me to watch events there with a keener interest than most.

It paid off. Fresh in my devotion to the operational catechism, and jealously solicitous about the "ugly duckling" character of my area by division standards, I snapped at the first signs of an emerging Soviet presence in the "Pearl of the Antilles." I had the good fortune to be assigned as secretary and aide a young woman who had some knowledge of Cuba, and we both knocked ourselves out to cover every manifestation of Soviet incursion into Cuba. Overnight we became the "experts." Ours became the official Agency list of the Soviets in Cuba, researched for biographic details and culled for known or suspected Russian Intelligence Service* (RIS) officers.

We had a rare opportunity to work in the innards of the Soviet division on its reason for existence — responsibility for the activities of Soviets anywhere in the world. In the abbreviated terminology of intelligence, that reduces to the Soviet "presence," a handy way to refer to the target. It is tangible, and when coupled with the prevailing assumption of its hostile character, it is an effective embodiment of the "foreign enemy," a surefire rallying cry for all-out resistance. In that vein we on the desk approached the problem, the more excited and motivated because the phenomenon was taking place in a country only ninety miles from the shores of the United States.

I brought to the job a rather extensive background on the subject of counterintelligence (CI) through case studies and research on the RIS. The latest case of which I had made a definitive study was that of Colonel Rudolf Ivanovich Abel of the Committee of State Security of the RIS. Abel, who was later traded back to the Soviets for the captured United States U-2 pilot Gary Powers, was widely publicized as the most important Soviet spy ever captured in America. He was the leading example of what was known in intelligence parlance as an "illegal," because he had no official or diplomatic status but passed as a citizen of the country he was operating in. My own study of that case had left me unimpressed with the caliber and performance of the RIS in the field. That tiny wedge of doubt about the omnipotence of the Russian Intelligence Service, of the foreign directorates of both the KGB and the GRU, was to grow as I became familiar in my new job with intelligence operations of both Soviet services. And it caused me to look askance at some of the prevailing orthodoxy within the Soviet division itself concerning our own CI operations and

*The term used in the CIA to denote the two Soviet intelligence services, the Committee of State Security (KGB) and the (military) Chief Intelligence Directorate (GRU). Reference to either service of the RIS will be to its *foreign directorate*, unless otherwise noted.

operational personnel.

Ever since my association with the Soviet division I had been led to believe that the elite component within the division was counterintelligence. The CI groups were the repository of the know-how necessary to deal with and to thwart what was generally considered the most advanced, most sophisticated, most numerous, and most ruthless intelligence service in the world, the RIS. To meet a conceived threat of such dimensions to the vital interests of the United States required of the CIA that it build its own assets to equal or surpassing strength, sparing no expense in the process. The inescapable logic of the endeavor was to depict the opposition service as expanding in numbers, funding, expertise, and operational cunning. Indeed, a succession of Directors in their periodic visits to Congress to justify their budget requests laid great stress on the accomplishments of the RIS.

For many of those with a personal stake in the CI build-up — case officers, intelligence analysts, file clerks, but especially case officers operating against the RIS in the field — the RIS was considered as an outfit composed of supermen "nine feet tall." Its foremost adversaries, the division's CI case officers, by being pitted against the best, were correspondingly accorded the status of being the best within the division. Indisputably, they had a corner on the market of knowledge of the organization and functions of the RIS and of its methods of operation which they copied and developed as their own. The exploits of some of our own CI case officers in the field became almost legendary, and as a group they earned the reputation of being the most proficient "operators" within the Clandestine Services.

It rapidly became apparent that the Latin American desk was subject to pressures from quarters outside the Soviet division. A persistent influence was exerted by the counterintelligence staff of the Clandestine Services. The CI staff was "gung ho" on the international communist conspiracy theory, with the added twist that they were convinced that there existed an unholy alliance between the RIS and the Communist Party of the Soviet Union in prosecution of that conspiracy. The CI staff was thoroughgoing in its research and documentation of the subject, and its coverage of communism on a worldwide scale was second to none. As "referent" on communism, the CI staff was required to coordinate and sign-off on all CI matters communicated from the desk to the field. More often than not there was an adversary relationship between the operations desk and CI staff, accompanied by delaying differences of opinion, jealousies over prerogatives, and hassles over compromises — satisfactory to neither side.

Philosophically, at the time I fell somewhere between the ideologically blinded anti-communists and the naive, equally blinded, apologists for communism. In other words, I had neither irrational hate nor fear of communism, and had since my student days at the College of the City of New York rejected the shallow tenets of Marxism. Still, on the level of practical politics, I had not disassociated the behavior of the Soviet Union from the sticky tenets of theoretical communism. I would admit to myself, but never to others, that I was only half convinced my job put me in the front lines against an implacable foe. Still, there was enough righteousness in my stance to lend wings to my efforts to accomplish the division's mission.

As 1959 wore on, the reports from Cuba became more ominous for relations between Cuba and the United States. A stream of refugees, mostly middle-class Cubans, began to trickle into the United States. Cuban nationalist emphasis was manifesting itself in decidedly reckless affronts to large foreign business concerns. In mid-April, Fidel Castro's visit to Washington, possibly to bargain for economic help, turned out to be a bust. A final contest was taking place in Cuba between communist and non-communist factions, and the snub from the United States may have tilted the course of the Cuban Revolution and driven it inexorably toward more radical solutions, including Castro's decision to seek help from the Soviet Union.

By then the Soviet division was beginning to sit up and take notice. The Latin American desk was assigned another case officer, an old hand of European experience, with the unspoken understanding that he was to be co-equal in the running of the desk. A few months later, the first report came in of a Soviet freighter putting in to a Cuban port, and it was felt that a Soviet specialist should go to Cuba to check it out. I was picked for the assignment. The beginning steps, movements, and impressions of my first temporary duty (TDY) visit abroad match the experiences of many intelligence officers who have been schooled in the cloistered halls of their profession and then are put out "on the street." It should put to rest the popular notion of the urbane, suave, unflappable foreign agent who unfailingly knows his way around in strange new surroundings.

The day after my arrival in Havana I paid a courtesy call on the embassy, quite the proper thing for a "tourist" to do; but while there, I checked in with the CIA field station, which of course was not the way a bona fide tourist behaved, and I felt a twinge of uneasiness. I was then set free to try on my "cloak and dagger," disguised beneath the Brownie camera I carried ostentatiously suspended from my neck.

The balance of that day I spent learning the ropes, a process called "familiarization," part of the prescribed drill. I rode several bus lines to different parts of the city. I studied my maps en route. I spoke my halting Spanish with several passengers. I snapped a few pictures. I discovered that I was wearing too much clothing because, though winter was approaching at home, Havana was hot and moist. Quite unaware of the process, I was learning to act the part of a tourist.

At night, I roamed the streets, eager for the sights and sounds of the city. I found them. I was openly accosted several times by young ladies who asked in broken English if I didn't wish to share the pleasure of their company, which showed that they still remembered the good old days. The first twenty-four hours of my stay in "unfriendly" territory eroded ever so slightly the tenability of the theory that Cuba was being plunged into communism. A little bit of realism was breaking through.

By the following day, I had completely abandoned those

compulsive but guarded looks to the rear to see whether I was being followed (which, according to the book, is what any agent is supposed to avoid doing as second nature). I checked in again with my colleagues to get the benefit of their advice on how to handle the next day's trip to the port of Cárdenas.

In the afternoon I wandered down to Havána harbor, charmed and intrigued en route by the narrow streets of "Old Havána," and walked as close as I could to the wharves until blocked by signs to "Keep Out." At the harbor, I noticed the presence of armed guards — the *barbudos* (bearded ones) with guns slung under their armpits. In the evening I dined out at the Havána Hilton, where there was pronounced evidence of the Revolution: young, poor Cuban couples meandering through the plush interior; scatterings of *barbudos* throughout the lobby and along the corridors; and a concentration of displays of Castro, the 26th of July movement, and the accomplishments (or hopes) of the government for the people. But through it all, I, a representative, if scarce, American tourist, was treated in easy Cúban style as a welcome guest.

This trip taught me something at the outset about the people in Latin countries: the passport to friendliness with them is your attempt to use their language, no matter how massacred. Somehow it breaks down their reserve and lowers their guard toward the *norteamericano* who, I found, is not universally loved south of the border. On the other hand, when you run into a Latin who wants to try his English on you, it is best to go along and maintain a satisfying mix. Some case officers I have known, language purists, seem unable to recognize this elementary precept of how to win friends and influence people in Latin America.

It was a beautiful, lazy Saturday morning when I started out in my Avis rental car from Havána, bound for Cárdenas. The travel folders I had seen spoke glowingly about the coast highway to Matánzas and beyond, and well they might. The ride was sheer delight and over too soon as I coasted into Cárdenas at siesta time. Among the practically deserted streets I finally located a little hub of activity at a plaza, which must have been at the center of town. I parked the car, slung my

Brownie into place, and began to amble about looking for a taxi. The few people I passed acknowledged my *buenas tardes* and smiled in return. No hostility. No suspicious looks. And here I was within shouting distance of a Soviet ship.

I found my taxi. It was a horse-drawn carriage, stationed just off the plaza. Ignoring some slight pangs of hunger, I asked the driver if he would take me to the harbor and other sights. He agreed, and off we jogged through the town just as it was beginning to come alive after siesta. He took me directly to the harbor area, where, big as life, the Soviet ship loomed over the wharf. I asked the driver to wait, jumped out of the carriage, and strode out on the wharf to a point where I could take pictures. If anyone was perplexed, interested, or concerned, he certainly didn't show it. There were a few sailors on deck. I took their pictures, too, and waved at them. They waved back. It was the jolliest spy mission one could imagine.

Very satisfied with my work, I continued my sightseeing trip by carriage. From the driver I learned that the ship had been loading sugar. With that "mission accomplished" feeling, I enjoyed my drive back to Havana. I would stow the undeveloped film in the recesses of my suitcase, just in case.

The Havana I found when I returned that Saturday night was far different from the Havana I had left in the morning. And with good reason; it was the eve of the convention of the American Society of Travel Agents (ASTA), some two thousand travel people from seventy different countries who had descended upon Havana in the first year of the Revolution to whoop it up like in the Havana of old. Even though it was a little off the Soviet beat, I found it quite easy to think that maybe I could uncover a few operational opportunities among that mob, especially since Castro and the Cuban Tourist Commission were going all out to entertain ASTA in hopes of reviving the tourist trade. And I had in my mind, too, sketchy reports of a few Soviet characters whom I might be able to glimpse.

The convention opened on Sunday. I was in the thick of it. My per diem allowance, while hardly lavish, permitted me to join in the festivities and to flit from partying group to

Accountants Are Now Marketing Pros!

Business people are looking for more services from their accountants. We provide marketing messages-on-hold for accountants all over the country *and for their clients.* **Hold It Systems** is the *premier message-on-hold company* and we can inform your clients about all of the services you provide including your recommendation of messages-on-hold. Offer marketing services to your clients and use **Hold It Systems** to *tell everyone about your services.*

Call us at 1-800-236-4058, fax us at (419) 227-8210 or mail this card back to us. P . . . .

Hold it ™
SYSTEMS

P.O. Box 1869
Lima, Ohio 45802-1869

☐ Yes, I want a free custom demo.
My needs are ☐ immediate ☐ 3-6 months ☐ future use.

Name _____

Company _____

Address _____

City _____

State _____ Zip _____

Phone _____

Fax _____

E-mail _____

Number of phone lines _____

Name of phone system if known _____

_____

M&C 10/2001

partying group. It was in the bar of the Hilton, where else, that I found myself in the company of a young lady, a dark-haired Latin beauty, who made no bones about why she had sought me out. She said she was not a travel agent, and not in Havana for a joy ride, but had come from Venezuela for a purpose. I asked her what her purpose was. She answered by telling me that she knew that I was an American agent!

I fenced. I repeated my cover story about getting away from business cares for a week, and so on. She laughed, and waved her finger deprecatingly in the Latin manner to show that I was not telling the truth. How then, I relented, did she know that I was an agent? She confided indulgingly that it was easy, that she was trained to recognize her colleagues in espionage. She had noted at once that I was a fish out of water in this crowd, even though trying to blend. I wore no ASTA insignia. She had listened to my superficial conversations in which I was soliciting ASTA impressions of the new revolutionary Cuba. And being an anti-Castroite herself, she was determined that I get to know "the truth" about the Revolution so that I could pass it on to my superiors. We talked into the wee hours, I buying the drinks, and I noted on a scrap of paper some biographic details of the Venezuelan Mata Hari as well as a few of the more lurid stories of Castro's infamous exploits.

Shortly after the American Embassy opened on Monday, I spoke with the deputy chief of the Havana Station and recounted the whole story of the evening before. We ran a trace in the station files for the woman's name, with no luck. The deputy asked a few of the case officers whether they knew of this Venezuelan agent, by physical description or name. None did. I filled him in on the information about Castro that had been given to me. How did it sound? Was it new? Did it ring with reliability? The second-in-command at the station was not that informed that he could give me definite answers, but in his opinion, he said, I should continue my association with the woman. He warned me to be careful, because the convention was swarming with Castro's agents. And he told me to keep a careful reckoning of the "operational" money I spent for drinks, etc. so that I could claim reimbursement.

With the mission laid on, I spent the rest of the day enjoying myself in my cover role: swimming in the hotel pool, lounging around the pool for lunch and drinks, napping and reading in fits stretched out on a soft deck chair. Even as I relaxed in dogged pursuit of familiarization, intrigue intruded. Also living it up at poolside familiarizing themselves was a small group of East Germans who looked nothing like communists should, and therefore were undoubtedly spies. Amazing how Cuba Libres in the hot sun can set one to daydreaming.

That night I was with Mata Hari again, although this time she seemed to have developed an enormous thirst. Between drinks, she returned to her favorite subject — the brutal tortures devised by Fidel Castro. Suddenly she announced that she felt lucky and prevailed on me to go with her to the casino at the Hotel Nacional. After one play at the roulette wheel, with my money, she apparently became physically exhausted. She said she wanted a drink. We adjourned to the crowded barroom with its mass of humanity hunched over Lilliputian-sized tables, and she promptly passed out, face down on a tabletop which she completely covered with her dark hair. I had to get her out of that inferno — which I did. I begged her to tell me where she lived. She did. I hailed a taxi and took her home. The ride braced her slightly, and when we arrived at a small apartment hotel, she gravely planted a kiss on my forehead, wobbled out of the cab, and disappeared into the hotel. We hadn't even firmed up a meeting for the following night, which I told her was to be my last in Havana.

On Tuesday evening, after packing and getting everything ready for the next day's departure, I strolled over to the Havana Hilton and went to our usual meeting place. The Venezuelan bombshell wasn't there. I spent a little over an hour jostling among the crowds, and had just about decided to return to my hotel when I saw her, in animated conversation with two men who were plying her with drinks. I was edging warily around the little knot of which she was the center, when she spotted me and called out gaily for me to join her. She introduced me to the two Englishmen with whom she was conversing, and when their attention was momentarily engaged elsewhere, she pointed to their ASTA insignia which gave their names and the travel agency to which they belonged. As she did so she laughed out loud, and then told me in a whisper that these two fine gentlemen had not brought their wives to the convention. She gave me a big wink, and then resumed her conversation with them. I surreptitiously made note of their names, and after some suggestive banter about the gentlemen taking her on their excursion the next day to Varadero Beach or wherever, I left them.

When I got back to Headquarters, I wrote up my reports and put my records and film into routine processing, including name traces of all the people with whom I had had more than passing contact. The two gentlemen from England put the frosting on the cake. They turned out to be officers of the British Secret Intelligence Service, MI-6, who [eight words deleted] for whatever they had up their sleeves. The irony of the situation finally dawned on me − whatever the wiles of the Venezuelan beauty, I had turned over a live American "agent" to another intelligence service. I hoped the British service was as generous with expense accounts as was the CIA.

2

HAVANA FOLLOW-UP:
I See Fidel

THREE months later I was back in Cuba on another TDY. That may not have been a record as far as repeat TDYs go in the Clandestine Services, but it was close to a record for brevity of the interval before reentering a "hostile" country. For during those three months, Cuba had been taking on the coloration of deliberate hostility to the United States. In January 1960, United States Ambassador to Cuba Philip W. Bonsal had delivered a note protesting the Cuban government's seizure of property owned by United States citizens. President Eisenhower, in a news conference shortly thereafter, reiterated United States determination to protect the rights of United States citizens which "have been disregarded and in which redress under Cuban law is apparently unavailable or denied."

But more than the United States' corporate eye was on the Cuban gadfly, the eye of the CIA was on the Russian bear. How the CIA interpreted Fidel Castro and the Cuban Revolution may be gauged from testimony given by General C. P. Cabell, Deputy Director, to the Senate Internal Security Subcommittee on November 5, 1959. Cabell said that Fidel Castro was "not a Communist" but "certainly not anti-Communist." His "extreme policies . . . are being exploited by the Communists to the maximum extent." He had "delegated authority in key areas to persons known to be pro-Communists or who are susceptible to exploitation by Communist propaganda." Fidel's brother Raul and Ernesto (Che) Guevara were "strong friends of the Communist Party." The General said more, but it is already clear that he was mouthing nothing less than the long-standing ideological pitch of the Cold War attitude toward international communism.

We on the Latin American desk of the Soviet division assiduously plied our trade, piling up signs of the Soviet presence in Cuba. We received a report from Mexico that Soviet workers and technicians of the Soviet Exhibition on Science, Technology, and Culture which had been in Mexico City since November 1959 had gone to Cuba to prepare for a showing of the Exhibition there. A news item in *The New York Times* of February 1, 1960, stated that Anastas I. Mikoyan, Soviet First Deputy Premier, was going to Cuba on February 4 to open the Exhibition. In the Soviet division's lexicon, all the indications were there for a Soviet takeover of the island. To counter that, or at least to keep tabs on it, the division called upon their seasoned "Man in Havana" — me.

The prospect of coming to grips personally with the RIS, in their perceived role as advance men for the takeover process, heightened by the presence of important Soviets for whom the RIS had security responsibility, should have been sobering even to a seasoned case officer. But it wasn't. I find it hard to explain exactly why, but rather than feeling the slightest trepidation I champed to have a go at it. Possibly it was a mix of my skeptical attitude about security (which I suspected applied to Soviets also) and my ineradicable impression of an easygoing Cuba that could temper the flinty ruthlessness (I assumed) of the most dedicated RIS-nik.

On the first night of my arrival in Havana, February 5, I found a changed Havana Hilton. It was now called the Habana Libre and had a worn look. Its expansive panels of glass were smudged and dirty. The plush settees and chairs spread around the lobby were in disarray. Vases that had held luxuriant flowers were empty. The scene that greeted me, however, had anything but a decadent look. The citizens' army, teenage *barbudos* in their green uniforms, each packing a menacing-looking submachinegun, were dashing about. High excitement was in the air.

And then I saw the cause of it all — Fidel Castro, who suddenly materialized in the lobby near the reception desk for a brief moment of solitary splendor before he was swamped by his admirers. In that moment, and only for that moment, the Castro I saw was someone I shall never forget. He was dressed in a soft light brown uniform, spotlessly clean, its buttons and insignia shining brightly. His beard was trimmed and combed, his hair brushed and soft-looking. His face was startlingly white. If a halo had appeared over his head, I would not have been surprised. He looked the incarnation of Jesus Christ!

I asked of no one in particular on the fringe of the crowd, *"Porque está aquí, el lider máximo?"* Without turning to me, someone answered, *"El Ruso,"* and waved over his shoulder at the grand stairway that ascended from the lobby to the mezzanine floor. What incredible luck, I thought to myself. The maximum leader and the Soviet First Deputy Premier were going to meet in a matter of moments. I knew what I had to do.

The crowd trailed away as Castro made his way up the stairs, gesticulating, smiling, embracing those within reach. As soon as the pack thinned out, I bounded up the stairway, strode briskly between two files of armed *barbudos*, and found myself at the entrance to a room, the door of which was open. I walked in as nonchalantly as possible and quickly seated myself in the nearest row of seats, as the door closed behind me. I was in the first row, occupied by only one other person, James Reston of *The New York Times.*

To me it was an historic occasion: Fidel Castro and Anastas Mikoyan stood facing each other, smiling and shaking their heads. Then the palaver began, through interpreters. I could make out some of the Spanish (the Cubans talk rapidly and clip letters from their speech), but less of the Russian. What they said to each other, the flowery phrases of good will, friendship and cooperation, was of little consequence to me. I was thrilled by just being there.

The meeting between the Cuban and the Russian was brief. The two retired to an adjoining room. The door to the meeting room was thrown open, and I walked out unhurriedly, savoring the heady wine of success. I'm not sure just how I made it back to the Hotel Vedado.

In reporting the meeting to Headquarters via Havana Station's communication channels the next day, I tried to convey my impressions of both men, and I think I said of *El Ruso* something to the effect that Mikoyan could have been, and acted like, anybody's grandfather. I am certain that my description of the ease with which I entered the inner sanctum, past the armed squads, made no impression on the counterintelligence experts at Headquarters. But the experience implanted in me, just a little deeper, doubts, amounting almost to disdain, for the alleged security omniscience of the RIS. I couldn't shake the feeling that this kind of skepticism, contrary to all operational doctrine, made for a more facile, effective case officer.

After opening the Exhibition on February 5 and holding the cordiality meeting with Castro, Mikoyan pretty much disappeared from public view for the balance of his stay in Cuba, until he departed on February 13. During that time he concluded some far-reaching economic agreements: the purchase of five million tons of sugar over a five-year period, and the offer of a $100 million long-term credit at low interest. The meaningful news to the CIA, however, was that Mikoyan reportedly had said that the U.S.S.R. would supply military planes to Cuba and that diplomatic relations would be established very soon.

I spent the remainder of my TDY (about a week and a half) following three main pursuits. One was "familiarization," living up my cover, interspersed among the other two as often as possible. Another was several visits to the Soviet Exhibition of Science, Technology, and Culture, where I snapped pictures of everything in sight, and of everybody who looked remotely Slavic. I took a series of multi-angle shots of Sputnik, the Soviet space vehicle (which I had seen in the Exhibition when it played New York the previous summer). And finally, I maintained nightwatches at the Habana Libre, where most of the Soviet functionaries seemed to congregate. (I even practiced surveillance by following them out of the hotel and tracking them to whatever bar they were headed for.) It was all done in the spirit of good clean fun, and except for my familiarization highjinks, I could claim operational expenses incidental to the Exhibition and surveillance.

My freely clicking camera at the Exhibition stripped away another notion or two that I had about Soviet security. In the past I had written several studies about Soviet security practices. Historically, the Russians have gone to extreme lengths to preserve "security" — as far back as Tsarist days and the use of the Okhrana (the secret political police), and in modern times the old tried and true secret police methods. I could have written a doctoral thesis on RIS security, and yet, I might have missed a most significant conclusion.

The clicking of my little Brownie brought that conclusion into focus. Just as the Soviets targeted their own people and captive communist audiences for propaganda purposes, so it was with security. In Soviet eyes, the potential "enemies of the state" were not CIA "spooks" gallivanting about abroad, and certainly not ordinary citizens of a country no matter how hostile the country's posture. Look at the facts. Russian emigres were hunted down from the early days of the Bolshevik Revolution, and if considered dangerous enough to the Soviets were kidnapped or assassinated. Defectors had to go into hiding to escape the long arm of the RIS. Trotsky was assassinated in Mexico City, as the culmination of a prolonged operation perpetrated by the RIS and its agents. Only the most trusted Soviets are allowed out of the Soviet Union, and even for them, the RIS always details a security officer to accompany them or assigns a resident security officer to monitor their activities. The Soviet military forces are under constant scrutiny by Special Sections (OO) of the KGB (the latter, by the way, make up the notorious OO "Death to Spies" outfit that James Bond tangles with, out of abysmal ignorance that they have no foreign intelligence missions). Facts piled on facts led to one conclusion: Security is for Russians.

So the RIS couldn't have cared less that some snooping American was taking pictures all over the place. As for

Sputnik, it was suspended from supporting sidewalls in plain sight for anyone to see, or to photograph to his heart's content. I heard and read somewhere of a CIA operation that was pulled off with that same Sputnik (not in Cuba). As the story goes, in the dead of night a crew entered the Exhibition hall, detached the Sputnik from its moorings, removed it from the hall to a nearby place where it was minutely photographed inside and out, returned it to the hall, anchored it to its accustomed site, stole out of the hall, and were safely back in their beds — all in record time, and the Soviets none the wiser.

In intelligence annals, an operation like that rates the highest marks, and I am loathe to dash cold water on the exploit. Indeed, if I don't miss my guess, one of my closest associates was the case officer. But I am constrained to hazard an educated guess that if that Sputnik exhibit had *anything* in it that was worth keeping secret (which I doubt), Soviet security officers would have been sleeping in it around the clock, and a pack of hungry Russian wolfhounds would have surrounded it night and day.

When I returned to Washington and had my film developed, no one got excited about those close-up shots of Sputnik. Something else did cause a stir in the operationally minded division: the realization that the Soviets would be establishing diplomatic relations with the Cubans, and that it might behoove the division to put a Soviet specialist into Cuba in readiness for it.

3

TRACKING THE SOVIETS:
The Latin American Desk

BY late 1947, when the CIA was established, the lines of the Cold War between the United States and the Soviet Union were drawn. The official ideology of the West held that the Soviet Union and communism were synonymous, and that combined they were an aggressive, expansionist movement dedicated to the overthrow of the capitalist world. This was the credo handed to the CIA, and it became the governing philosophy of the Clandestine Services, which by the CIA's charter was the action arm of the new Agency.

The Office of Strategic Services (OSS), a predecessor of the CIA during World War II, had had relatively little experience with Russians or the RIS. Its methods of operation had grown out of the typical exigencies of a wartime situation, dealing mainly with problems of infiltrating agents and forming nets behind enemy lines, and delving into the manipulation of propaganda as a weapon. Both the methods and many of the personnel of OSS were the residual base from which the CIA, and in particular the Clandestine Services, were formed.

Close study of the opposition services by Headquarters intelligence officers, aided in the early days by the organizational data and case studies furnished by "allied" intelligence services, was the foundation in some degree for the construction of our own foreign intelligence system. At one time I taught a course in the CIA's Office of Training in which I compared the various organizational units of the Russian Intelligence Service (internal and foreign) to those elements of the "intelligence" complex that had been formed in the United States. The striking thing about the comparison was the diversity of separate organizations in the United States (Secret Service, Federal Bureau of Investigation, Office of Emergency Preparedness, United States Information Service, National Security Agency, self-contained security offices for the Atomic Energy Commission and other "sensitive" organizations, Central Intelligence Agency, etc.). For foreign intelligence alone, the model at hand was formidable.

Even though I was not present at the creation of the Clandestine Services of the CIA, I can't help thinking that the growing awareness on the part of CI officers of the size, complexity, and range of accomplishments of the foreign directorate of the KGB and of the lesser-known foreign directorate of the GRU inspired admiration and twinges of jealousy. It must have seemed that it would take superhuman effort to catch up. Yet, what evolved in skeletal form came about fairly rapidly. The bony structure of the Clandestine Services closely resembles that of the KGB foreign directorate: area operational divisions (the extremities); service, analytic processing, and personnel staffs (the support columns). Even though emulation might be the sincerest form of flattery, it seems that the early admirers went beyond that. By the time I arrived on the scene, I became distinctly aware of the attitude of seasoned CI case officers to regard the RIS not only as a tough elite organization but one composed of officers "nine feet tall."

The initial operational thrust of the Soviet division was closely in line with the OSS behind-the-lines model, although updated to "behind the iron curtain" objectives. The principal mission was to collect information on the Soviet Union and its people by secret means — best described as espionage. Information so collected went under the name of foreign intelligence or positive intelligence to distinguish it from information related to counterintelligence. In the early days of the CIA, the Soviet division mounted a major effort to penetrate the Soviet Union with border-crosser agents. After a few years the effort was all but abandoned, probably because of excessive difficulties and costly mishaps. That type of operation was a variation of the "illegal" operation, mentioned earlier in connection with Rudolf Abel, because its success depended on the agent's capability of passing as an ordinary citizen of society. The Soviet division then shifted to the "legal" operation, making use of persons who had "legal" or legitimate reasons to enter or leave the Soviet Union, in the first instance foreigners including Americans and in the second Soviets who were officially outside the Soviet Union.

It was already known, thanks to publicity from J. Edgar Hoover and the FBI, that Soviets abroad in embassies, consulates, and trade organizations, or even on temporary junkets and missions, were used by the RIS in carrying out espionage. Also, with convincing doctrinaire theorizing by J. Edgar Hoover to support it, it was widely believed that the RIS in league with local communists was making headway in subverting the United States and its allies. Included within the "threat" were those who were dubbed dupes, fronts, or "fellow travelers." How to deal with this spreading army?

The new approach, relying as it did on so-called "live sources" to cover the target, required rapid development of a wide screening process to uncover leads to prospective agents. In the period immediately following Stalin's death in 1953, a period of relative scarcity of interchange between the Soviet Union and the outside world, the number of candidates for recruitment was circumscribed. In a way, this was a boon because it permitted the division to develop and test the techniques that certainly would be required to meet successfully the demands of an expanded program. As the incidence of legal travel increased during the "thaw" under Khrushchev, the division could afford to become more selective in its agents destined for travel to the Soviet Union, and could consequently pay more heed to their caliber and the range of their access to targets within. Even for "live" Soviet targets on the outside, or for that matter within the Soviet Union, the more relaxed atmosphere augured well for greater ease in approaching them to elicit information.

"Legal" approach doctrine had been well established by the time I assumed my duties as an area operations desk officer. My background in the division as research analyst on the Soviet Union, and especially my experience at the National Security Agency as a communications analyst for the same area, were helpful in my accommodating readily to the legal travel concept.

4

OUR MAN IN HAVANA:
Keeping an Eye on the Soviets

THE Soviet division revved up its negotiations with the Western Hemisphere division in order to have their "Man" in Havana as soon as possible. In the meantime, while following events in Cuba attentively from the vantage point of the Latin American desk, I embarked on an after-hours conversational Spanish course at Berlitz (which the Agency paid for). Normally, the arrangements between divisions for a person being sent abroad would result in a permanent change of station (PCS) assignment, with all that that signified in the way of employee emoluments and perquisites, including accompaniment of family or dependents. But, evidently because of the "precarious" situation in Cuba, a compromise arrangement was worked out. It called for a three-month TDY, under cover as a "temporary" employee of the State Department, with per diem allowance, but no family; and the Soviet division retained the option to continue its representation by a replacement after the three-month period.

One seldom argued with the decrees or judgments from above; the Clandestine Services operated along the lines of a semi-military model. There was nothing so precise as army regulations on soldierly behavior, but it was understood that in a front line outfit one accepted the discipline of the military code. That accounts as much as anything for the myth that our "spies" are willing to suffer tight-lipped martyrdom. At any rate, when the nature of the Cuba assignment was spelled out for me, I did not reject it. I managed to soften the estrangement from my family by getting the authorities to agree to a brief home "vacation" during the period, and a visit to Cuba by my wife if the situation permitted. On that basis, I left for Cuba on May 24, 1960, less than three weeks after the establishment of formal diplomatic relations between the U.S.S.R. and Cuba.

Because I was no stranger to Cuba, no one of the Havana Station was on hand to welcome me at José Martí Airport. I had decided against staying at the Hotel Vedado, much as I liked it, because I had been known there before as a tourist. So, after a one-night stand at a second-rate hotel, I went about the city searching for a "residence." I tried one of the swankiest hotels in Havana, the Capri, and struck a deal with the management (a cheaper rate for embassy personnel) which really put me up in style. I was to live in that hotel (featured in the movie "Our Man in Havana"), with its rooftop swimming pool, its gambling casino, lavish night club, bars, and Skippy's Hideaway Coffee Shop (which tried valiantly to live up to its reputation during belt-tightening times), for nearly two months, including the three weeks my wife spent in Havana for our umpteenth honeymoon.

Working within a field station is not something to be learned from CIA regulations, and I was lacking a slight assist in that direction because, unlike most officers who are sent abroad for the first time, I had not undergone the relevant Clandestine Services training course. Even by the end of my tour, there was much I had not assimilated of the complexities of a working station. I will outline its organization and functions, necessary for an understanding of how I, the "outlander," was to fit in.

The organizational chart looks something like the following (which, by the way, is strikingly similar to the overseas *Rezidentura* of the KGB):

Chief of Station

Deputy Chief of Station

Operations	Support	Administration
Case Officers	Reports Officers	Administration Officers
Counterintelligence	Communications, or "Commo" Officers	Clerks
Positive Intelligence		
Covert Actions	Technicians, usually TDY	
Propaganda		
Political Action		
Special Targets		
Assistants/Typists		

The Chief of Station does all the high-level wheeling and dealing. In a normal situation, the chief engages in government-to-government liaison with functionaries of the host country, in those fields that are outside the province of State Department protocol (the Station Chief is nominally accountable to the ambassador). The Deputy Chief often takes over liaison with the police and intelligence organizations of the host country. At the operational level, there is a cadre made up of case officers, whose responsibilities are divided by their operational specialties or the targets they cover. The local targets in most instances are the indigenous Communist Party, front organizations, leftist groups, radical elements (of universities, etc.), and anti-government movements. Other case officers (often by request from the station) are assigned to the non-local priorities such as the Soviets, Chinese communists, or others from communist countries. In some countries with large communist country representation, entire sections of the station may work on these non-local target obligations. But it must be remembered that Havana Station was in a hostile, non-cooperative country.

The typical station's support apparatus consists of the following elements: the reports officer, who extracts information of general value from case officer reports and processes it in report form to Headquarters; operational aides and typists (often combined in the same person) to assist case officers; housekeeping for the entire station, done by an administrative staff which, besides being a small counterpart of the Department of Health, Education, and Welfare for all personnel and their dependents, also disburses and audits the finances for operations; the communications officer ("Commo"), to maintain the Agency's codes and operate its channel of communications to Headquarters. In larger stations, there may be "technicians" for on-the-spot photographic or electronic operational duties, surreptitious entry, and so on.

Havana Station, although preoccupied with its local concerns, accepted me with open arms. I was given a desk and assigned one of the scarce aide/typists, a young woman who, fortunately, was a venturesome soul and provided invaluable assistance in operations from time to time. Most important, since I had neither the established roots nor the time for selective recruiting, the other case officers went out of their way to give me the benefit of their own agents' contribution to my problem. In several instances, case officers relinquished their agents to me when needed. The chief and the deputy chief were accessible at all times and most helpful in getting me over the rough spots. And the support staff was magnificent in aiding my adjustment.

The CIA's Havana Station, of course, was not identified as such within the American Embassy. Yet, as with every bureaucracy, the word got around. Despite my cover as a temporary employee of the State Department, I was nevertheless pegged early on as a CIA man. The station works closely with the component parts of the embassy: the military attachés, the legal attaché (FBI), trade, labor, and especially political and press sections. CIA people enjoy an "elite" reputation within the embassy community, although sometimes the deference may be grudging and lead to friction with other elements of the embassy. Nevertheless, the embassy is in a sense one big family, and the CIA fits in closely among the social and recreational activities that are a constant of embassy life.

5

FIRST OPERATIONS:
Trailing Russians in Cuba

ALTHOUGH the bloom of being on the team of the station was not to wear off for my entire stay, after having learned where the nearest men's lavatory was, where the No. 2 pencils were kept, and what kinds of files the station maintained, I was about ready to tackle the serious business of being a spy. Without agents of my own, I was constrained to do the next best thing: to reinforce other station case officers' understanding of the scope of the Soviet problem and to establish liaison with informational sources within the embassy, primarily with the military attachés. The latter were particularly necessary for directing walk-in informants to the right people.

Being agent-less meant I had to be my own "agent." Besides the promise of living a more exciting operational life, I would also be out on the street, rubbing elbows with the people, continuing the bash of familiarization that I not only enjoyed but that I felt exposed me to a deeper appreciation of the realities in Cuba. I continued my Spanish lessons three nights a week at the Berlitz school, with a serious-minded woman instructor (a former school teacher who had visited the United States) who often discussed with me the significance and meaning of Castro's Revolution. I mingled with Cubans, listened to their complaints, was caught up in their enthusiasms, and savored through elbow-to-elbow osmosis the flavor of their lives. I also talked often with those persons who formed long lines every working day at the embassy, waiting and hoping to flee with their exit visas the country they loved.

27

More to the point of acting like a case officer, I proceeded with the task at hand: the identification of the Soviets in Cuba. In accordance with the theory that the RIS was the advance party for digging in the Soviets, my first efforts were along those lines. I followed the outstandingly likely conduits to RIS activity: RIS contact with the local Communist Party and the absolute necessity of the RIS to set up secure communications with the homeland.

The information from my fellow case officers who were zeroed in on the Cuban communist party (the Popular Socialist Party) unearthed just enough of a lead on one Soviet who had been in contact with the party to give me a starting point for investigation. It was a lucky hit. The Soviet (whom I shall call Aleksandr), once singled out, proved from other source reporting to have been a very peripatetic fellow who had shown up at various places in Havana. Where to go from there? Even spot-checking those places by personal surveillance would have sapped all my energies.

Then there was another timely break, which emerged in the manner of a mystery. Evidently the International Cable Service in Havana had in its possession some strange messages in code (I believe they were five-digit groups) that were being sent from Havana to Moscow, and these were brought to the attention of the American Embassy. (I shall not say in what manner or by whom. I wish to make plain that one security breach about the past that I deem consequential is to reveal identifiable data about agents which, in turn, might lead to their compromise even now.) The messages had been delivered to the Cable Service from a particular address, which also appeared on the list of places frequented by the meandering Aleksandr.

The Beach House Operation

I immediately dubbed this new development "the beach house operation" because that was the description of the location at which Aleksandr had been seen. Many a hot, sunny afternoon I spent parked within viewing distance of the beach house. Once or twice, I saw Aleksandr going in or coming out. He always was on foot. For all my watching, I was unable to determine whether he lived there. I also caught glimpses of other men of Slavic appearance around the house, but I was never close enough to get a decent physical description. At least, I had established that some of the Soviets in Cuba were living in that house.

Aleksandr became my pet project. Of an evening when I had nothing else to do, or had finished my session of conversational Spanish at Berlitz, I would drop over to the Habana Libre. Every so often, Aleksandr would appear there; for what purpose I could only guess since I always spotted him alone, and always wearing sports clothes, which seemed to be his only attire night or day. When Aleksandr left, I followed him out into the night. More likely than not he would take the same walking route back to a hotel that was just down the corner from the Hotel Vedado. Of course, that settled the question of where Aleksandr lived. And the fact of his being separated from his colleagues added something to his stature.

I always went through the recommended motions of surveillance, keeping my distance, keeping him in sight, crossing the street from time to time, moving when he paused — but from all that I learned only where he lived. I never saw him in the company of another Soviet on his strolls. I never knew whether he saw me in his company.

Aleksandr must have been a loner in his dealings with the Popular Socialist Party, too. We never learned who it was he contacted within the party. Even if we had, we could only have speculated about its significance. The days were long gone since the RIS relied on activists of the communist party underground to carry out espionage or sabotage, or even the simplest support tasks. Further, there was no point to that in Cuba. Given the delicate relationship between the Cuban communist party and Fidel Castro's regime, Aleksandr's duties at PSP headquarters may have been to bludgeon the party into line with Castro. That would have been the way for the U.S.S.R. to impress the Cuban government. At the time, however, we did not give the RIS credit for doing the sensible thing.

We assumed that Aleksandr and the other Soviets were conducting themselves with the full knowledge of the Cuban government — even though before the arrival of Soviet diplomats that might have had to be publicly obscured. Quite likely, the RIS chief and his assistants were working hand in glove with Cuba's security force. The RIS, indeed, would characteristically have attempted to penetrate the security force of its friendly host, which at the time was the Cuban Army Intelligence Service (G-2). I have no doubt that the RIS wasted no time in trying to instill Soviet security practices into the Cuban G-2 — as much for the protection of Soviet personnel and activities in Cuba as for the objectives of the Cuban regime.

About all that can be said of the presumed Soviet attempt to dominate or manage Cuban security forces is that no hard evidence of it came to light, at least during the period I was in Cuba. And if the Soviets were indoctrinating and training the Cuban G-2 in the classic practices of security, Soviet style, all I can say further is that the impact of it was little recognized or felt at the foreign operational level. Cuban G-2 was adept at seizing upon superficial reasons or trumped-up reasons for denouncing foreigners that they wished to stigmatize, but that reflected little expertise on their part. Perhaps the vaunted security of the Cubans, as I have suggested for the Russians, lay in their capacity to deal effectively with Cuban nationals (within and without) and threats to the regime.

To sum up. The "beach house" was the first solid link in the chain which, when coupled with the other links such as Headquarters identification of Aleksandr as a known officer of the KGB, his solo contact with the communist party, his association with secret communications to Moscow, and his ubiquitousness on the Havana scene led to the conclusion that we had the chief *Rezident* of the RIS in Cuba squarely in our sights. But beyond being an impressive entry in a counterintelligence record book, there is really little more to having identified the man in the job. If Aleksandr had not been found, he would have had to be invented, or presupposed.

The fruits of espionage that might have ripened from the

beach house operation, and I mention only the most luscious — discovering what Aleksandr was talking about with Cuban communist party leaders, unearthing a key to his coded messages to Moscow, learning what he may have imparted to Cuban political leaders or security forces, determining what steps he was taking to counter American intelligence, discerning the assets he was installing in Cuba to advance espionage against the United States — were not forthcoming, and were not likely to bloom late. About the most that can be said about Aleksandr, apart from his being a nice chap whom I enjoyed tailing around Havana, is that we knew of his KGB affiliation when a few years later he became the Soviet Ambassador to Cuba. It's a safe bet that he didn't get the job just because he was down in the record books of the CIA.

The Soviet Shipping Operation

An important area of sustained information-seeking operations concerning the Soviet presence was Soviet shipping. Initial interest in the subject by the Clandestine Services probably stemmed from Mikoyan's quoted remark that the Soviets would deliver military supplies to Cuba. In any event, my focus of interest was not on arrivals or departures of Soviet ships, but on what militarily significant supplies they were delivering and where those supplies were being deployed. Since the military attachés (Naval, Army, and Air) had the resources and the sources for that kind of raw information, I made the necessary arrangements to tap into their feeder lines. I dutifully reported to Headquarters what seemed to me to be of unusual interest, although it was duplicative of what the attachés were reporting to their services.

In retrospect, it seems to me that the CIA missed a good bet. That bugaboo "security" did not permit reporting case officers to know that the Agency was actively planning a military invasion of Cuba. A 1974 study of Cuba under Castro notes that in March 1960 President Eisenhower instructed the CIA to draw up contingency plans for an exile invasion.* The

---

Cuba Under Castro: The Limits of Charisma, Edward Gonzalez, Houghton Mifflin Company, Boston, 1974, p. 75.

case officers at Havana Station were the last to know (aside from possibly the chief, his deputy and a "political action" case officer or two). Even though the Cuban press played the theme of the invasion loud and often, that was not the same as getting it from the horse's mouth; and worse was not being able to assist intelligently in the development of the plan.

A serious deficiency in intelligence collection crops up when the case officer, who does the collecting, lacks guidance from the Center, which monitors "the big picture." How is a case officer to know of his own reporting what is important or what is drivel; what should be dropped or, more important, what should be pursued more strenuously; what should be the order of priorities for collection within his own range of capabilities? The only mechanism that provides any sort of guidance is at best a delayed reaction that comes in the form of the case officer's published and distributed "report" (if it is published), which makes its way back to the station among other published reports. But, as any frustrated reports officer at Headquarters can tell it, the slipshod system doesn't work.

Presumably, compartmentalization is required because the enemy lurks everywhere — even in the very bowels of the intelligence establishment. The handmaidens to compartmentalization are personnel and physical security, both of which have been reduced to ritualistic procedures for the safeguarding of secret information or secret materials. The principle of "need to know" is rigidly enforced with respect to substantive information. Its rationale is constantly upheld in periodic reminders and hardhitting indoctrination courses. Physical security is more demonstrably visible — in such practices as double-checking locked safes; dropping secret-trash bags down chutes directly into incinerators; guarding checkpoints for entry and exit of employees; and so on. Infractions of the rules are called "violations," and may carry penalties up to dismissal.

The implication of these measures is that individual employees are not to be trusted. Few employees go so far as to consider the lack of faith degrading; but there are relatively few among the older hands who do not chafe under security measures, mock them, ignore them, or regard them as farcical.

Still, attitudinal reactions are the least of the problem; much worse is the totally unrealistic philosophy that there can be effective security under the blanket risk concept. Nothing short of a security tool that could pierce and monitor an individual's mind to spot dishonest intentions offers the slightest protection. Locked safe-drawers, "need-to-know" dissemination lists, or isolation of compartmentalized personnel are vulnerable to the unsuspected, determined, resourceful person bent on circumventing them.

The more irrational outcome is that compartmentalization actually vitiates and undermines the intelligence process. In the Clandestine Services compartmentalization seems to be carried on mindlessly. A few examples. Operations-support people (analysts and researchers) are blocked from knowing essentials of operations critical for supplying the fullest measure of data, advice, or criticism. Case officers working their own operations do not trade information with one another, though they surely would profit from mutual consultation, if on no other basis than that two heads are better than one. Defectors seem to be regarded as the private property of their operational handlers, whereas the ready access of research analysts to assist in debriefing would likely produce more comprehensive and reliable information. "High-level" information, that is to say, the product of politically or operationally sensitive operations, is so restricted in its dissemination as to raise the question of whether it is worth the risk.

The most guarded confines of compartmentalization are reserved for agents. The identity and characteristics of clandestine agents are held so close to the chest, or are so altered and disguised as the source for reports, that the very people who must know about the agent in order to evaluate his information are deprived of that essential insight. Why must the agent be so completely buried from sight? The reason given is to protect him against "compromise" — a chain result that presumably emanates from an inside employee to some outside confederate, or to some undetermined authority that might put the agent in jeopardy of life or limb. The scenario strains probability and good casting. The greater probability and more likely possibility is that agents will compromise themselves through ineptness or in routine performance of their duties in those areas where the watchful attentions of authority are everpresent.

I still have remorse over what might have been in connection with a report I recall vividly. Informers were providing the attachés with reports of the cargoes being off-loaded from the Soviet freighters, and often included supplementary information about destinations of the shipments. The report that stands out in my mind was one that gave a convincing description of smaller-type armaments (by the size, weight, shape, and characteristic crating of the ensemble) that could have been anti-aircraft equipment. That particular lot, according to the informer, was going to be dispatched to Bahía de Cochinos (The Bay of Pigs). It was an item of information I recall reporting to Headquarters.

My point is not that Headquarters should have done handsprings when the information was received. But if the Bay of Pigs was looming up in contingency planning as a possible landing site for the invading forces (whether at that particular stage of planning or later, when "Bay of Pigs" should have popped out from the information retrieval system), there should have been a request to the station to follow through on the report on a priority basis, to verify or confirm it, to amplify it, or to discredit it. Whatever the results concerning the reliability of the report, it might, just might, have influenced the planning.

Perhaps Headquarters, in its wisdom, did well not to keep the Havana Station case officers clued in too closely to what was going on. If they had, we might have spent sleepless nights over the realization that the Cubans, the Soviets, and the rest of the world seemed to know perfectly well what was in the offing.

6

DEFECTOR INDUCEMENT:
The Ship Captain Operation

WHEN the "legal travel" concept was adopted in the Soviet division and became a viable program in the mid-1950s, the possibility existed, at least in theory, that Soviets within the Soviet Union or temporarily abroad might be reached. This gave rise to intelligence's most splendid dream — the defection or recruitment of an agent "in place." By the same token, it was recognized that so venturesome and risky an operation had to be worth the candle. Consequently, there was a shift of emphasis toward a new set of targets, those Soviets who carried important knowledge in their heads or had access to the knowledge.

The operational approach to Soviets of this higher order necessarily had to be modified, both in terms of the techniques of recruitment and, if successful, in terms of communications. The virtual one-shot contact opportunity, coupled with limited exposure time, might as a practical necessity reduce a recruitment attempt to the so-called "cold approach." That means cornering your man and putting the question of his collaboration directly to him. While your target is in a mild state of shock, you thrust on him prepared instructions for subsequent contact. The chances were that the Soviet would keep the advances made to him to himself, rather than divulge them to Soviet authorities, which might jeopardize his travel abroad, or worse. He might brood over the advantages of cooperation and opt for it. At any rate, a seed would have been planted, and no one could tell when it might blossom. Nothing ventured, nothing gained. If recruited, the matter of communications presented formidable obstacles, particularly if the Soviet remained in the Soviet Union. Case officers, specially groomed for "in-place" operations, worked on both phases of the program. The Soviets are painfully aware of the most celebrated "in-place" operation of the century, that of Colonel Oleg Penkovskiy, a highly placed GRU officer who conveyed information of extreme importance from the Soviet Union. Penkovskiy is still "in place" — but dead.

The Ship's Captain Operation

At this point in my career I had never had a face-to-face encounter with a Russian, but one lazy morning while gratefully soaking up the cool air of the office, I found myself dumped onto the treadmill of a classic defector-inducement operation. From the moment the visa section of the embassy gave notice that a Soviet ship's captain was applying for a United States transit visa and would be appearing at the embassy that very afternoon, I fell into the holding pattern that governs all such opportunities. I agreed at once to take over, much to the relief of the visa section, which assumed that Soviets were the CIA's baby anyway.

There was much to do in preparing to confront the Soviet. First, I sent off an expedite cable to Headquarters for traces on the self-designated *kapitan*, giving the only information I knew — his name and his ship. I was banking on the Soviet division's impressive defector-inducement file to come up with a hit on so prominent a traveler as a ship's captain.

It is a cliche in the intelligence world that an intelligence service is no better than its files. The Soviet division's most impressive array of weaponry for meeting the threat of hordes of RIS-niks was the card file system devised for Soviets abroad. Every scrap of information from open and secret sources was distilled onto these personnel cards — from Soviet ambassador down to embassy cook, from prima ballerina of the Ballet Russe to the oboist in the pit of the orchestra. A constant check was maintained, by reference to recognizable criteria, to categorize persons as known or suspected intelligence officers of the RIS. A never-ending search was conducted of all the data to unearth any telltale signs of "vulnerability" — those factors in a personal history that might be used to "induce" (blackmail, pay off, sway, etc.) someone to come over to our side. There were many solid statistical uses to which the files were put, but the name of the game was "defector inducement."

More specialized than the "defector inducement" files, but no less important, were the files for counterintelligence. They constituted the working files of the CI groups within the division, one for KGB (the "civilian" intelligence service), the other for GRU (the military intelligence service), both of which had components which were engaged in foreign intelligence. The listings of known and suspected RIS officers abroad (taken from the "defector inducement" file) were combined with information on members of the two intelligence services (gained principally from defectors) to provide as complete a roster as possible of the personnel of the KGB and GRU. Information processed from these files was blended with information about the organizational components of the two Russian services to reconstruct their profiles. Knowledge of their profiles in turn helped to flesh out the nature of their functions, which, at least for foreign intelligence, were reinforced by observations and reports of CIA case officers in the field.

For the six years I worked as a research analyst within the division, I was well acquainted with the "counterintelligence" and "defector inducement" files and knew of those Soviet defectors who had come over to our side. I often worked intimately with the material derived from debriefing these individuals. Yet I never once dwelt on the connection between the files and the defector, nor had any of my colleagues raised the point. Rather, there was a tendency in the minds of the uninitiated, those who had no "need to know" of operations, that the very denial of information to them only confirmed that the fine hand of an operation was responsible. Later, much later, when the mystique of operations had dissolved, I came to recognize the reality: that "defector inducement" was a myth; that the prodigious investment in this program was a bust. Any defector that I ever heard of had turned himself in (a "walk-in") of his own volition, and on his own initiative.

The Soviet ship's captain was one of these walk-ins. The mechanics for the meeting were relatively simple to arrange, with the visa section eager to give me whatever I asked. At the appointed hour I would slip into the visa section and occupy one of the desks for interviewing applicants. I was briefed by a visa section clerk on the normal procedures for conducting an interview, and provided with an application form (in English and Spanish) which was to be filled in by the interviewer. The visa clerk, unable to restrain bureaucratic apprehension, suggested that if a transit visa were to be issued, it would be best to call in a clerk to complete the procedure. I was happy to agree, because conflicting thoughts were already beginning to sully my expectation of that cherished moment when I would offer asylum to the *kapitan*.

One such conflict bubbled up to the surface with an almost audible pop — suppose the *kapitan* spoke only Russian. I had a reading ability in Russian which had been sufficient for the supportive research I had done previously. But I couldn't speak Russian much beyond *do svidaniya* or *spasibo*. It had never dawned on me that the only time a case officer would have to speak Russian was when he was face to face with a Russian who could speak nothing else. I was aware, of course, that the Soviet division handled Russian defectors and that the handlers were the top-notch Russian speakers of the division. I now began to understand why, in the informal pecking order of the division, Russian-speaking case officers were accorded first place and the highest regard.

I hurried to my Russian dictionary and painstakingly looked up Russian equivalents for the entries on the application form. If the conversation with the *kapitan* became more involved, I would have the dictionary at my side and I resolved that he and I would understand one another no matter how tortuous the process. A man's life was not something with which you played a semantic game of Russian roulette.

I leaned back in my tilt-chair and considered various scenarios. The basic question had to be: "Why would a Soviet leave Cuba for the United States?" If the Soviet merely meant to get back to the Soviet Union, there were any number of ways: for a ship's captain, there was his own ship, or there were other Soviet vessels sailing from Cuba, or planes from Europe which were arriving and departing José Marti airport with increasing frequency. There was only one logical answer, or at least it was an answer that would have to be logically assumed as a starting point for a meaningful approach — the *kapitan* was bolting.

Knowing as much as I did about Soviets who tried to wiggle outside the Iron Curtain, I had to expect that the *kapitan* was in a high state of alarm. At any moment, some burly Soviet security guard or KGB-nik might burst onto the scene. Even at that very moment, the *kapitan* might be under lock and key. I felt a mounting nervousness: What would I do if he didn't show up? Investigate his whereabouts? I knew his ship was tied up in Havana Harbor, but what could I do about it? I had to shut out the unpleasant possibility that his defection intentions had been discovered by the Russians.

I was determined not to tip my hand when the *kapitan* showed up, but to allow him to make the play. I dug out of the files the Clandestine Services guidance on the procedures for handling walk-in defectors seeking asylum — procedures with which responsible embassy officials were also presumably familiar. The regulations called for periodic joint CIA/embassy reviews of the rules governing defectors, and I silently prayed that the last one had not been in the too-distant past. During my subsequent service under official cover in Cuba, and later in Mexico, I heard not once that such meetings took place; confident at the time, however, I reviewed the guidance with an eye to the protocol that must be observed when a political refugee sought asylum in the United States.

The review brought back to mind a celebrated defection with which I was thoroughly familiar, since I had written the definitive account of it for the Clandestine Services. It was the defection of a KGB illegal agent, named Hayhanen, in Paris, which broke the case of spy-master Rudolf Ivanovich Abel wide open. The Federal Bureau of Investigation got the credit for the remorseless tracking down of Abel, but that wasn't the case at all.

It was CIA people in Paris who did a remarkable job of landing Hayhanen and delivering him to the United States. (Incidentally, every rule in the book on defector reception was broken.) Hayhanen, by the time he reached Paris en route from the United States to the Soviet Union on leave, was a raving lunatic. He had good cause to reach a breaking point, because as an assistant to the illegal *Rezident* Abel he had done an abominable job. He had married a Finnish woman even before being dispatched to the United States to serve with Abel, and had committed the unforgiveable sin of keeping that knowledge from Abel and the security-minded KGB. After his wife had joined him in the United States, the two of them became rank lushes. With all that on his mind, and being officially recalled to the Soviet Union, he went berserk in Paris.

He initiated a telephone call to the U.S. Embassy, mumbling who he was to a clerk, and may even have come around to the embassy but without remaining long enough for CIA case officers to get on to him. Nevertheless, somewhere along the way he left an address where he could be found. The story after CIA officers made contact is unbelievable.

Getting Hayhanen to a "safe house" where he could be debriefed was a nightmare. From time to time he would strike a pose as a transmitter, arm raised like an antenna, and rattle out messages in Russian. He babbled about his wife back in the United States. He had to be plied incessantly with liquor, just to keep his level of violence down. He did produce some documentary evidence of his role as a spy in the United States, but could give his debriefers little coherent information of his activities. But he did pinpoint the whereabouts of his superior, Abel. The CIA officers realized that they were on to something hot, and arranged to transport Hayhanen back to the

United States. The case officer who accompanied him on the commercial plane deserves a medal for getting Hayhanen and himself back in one piece. When they reached the United States, the FBI was there to greet them, and took over.

The FBI swooped down on Abel's photography shop in Brooklyn, arrested him, and uncovered a layout of spy paraphernalia that staggered the mind (and overly stimulated the FBI and CIA to accord Abel the rank of greatest and most important spy ever caught): hollowed-out pencils and coins for storing microfilm messages, microdot apparatus, radio transmitters and receivers, codebooks, photographs, etc. Rudolf Abel, a man in his sixties, was tried in a Federal court, found guilty, and sentenced to a long prison term. Not once, to the best of my knowledge, during interrogation by the FBI before trial or later in prison, did he breathe a word about his activities. From my study of the case, despite what I have already said about Abel's limited accomplishments as spymaster, I grew to admire his personality and character, his warm regard for his family, and his resolute courage. I was happy to learn of his release, in exchange for Gary Powers. When he returned to Russia, he joyfully rejoined his family, received the Order of Lenin medal, and reportedly led a fruitful life until his death in the early 1970s. Hayhanen, under protection of the FBI, drank himself into an early grave.

With thoughts of the touch-and-go defection of Hayhanen swirling around in my head, and with only the original information about the *kapitan* to go on, I went to the visa clerk's office at the appointed hour. From my position at the desk, on which I had spread the application form and laid my Russian dictionary, I gazed out of the glass partition toward the large waiting room where my man was presumably sitting. I was ready for the big moment.

A clerk called the *kapitan*'s name. A short, slight, elderly man with a weatherbeaten face and snow-white hair arose from the bench and walked steadily to the swinging gate of the guard-rail. He entered the door of my office, and sat in the chair facing the desk to which I pointed. I gulped, glanced around nervously to see whether I was the focus of all eyes in the visa section, and then bent rigidly to the application form before me. In Russian, I put the first question — *"Nazvaniye?"* — meaning "Your name?" The *kapitan* replied promptly. I next ventured the Russian word for "birthplace" or "citizenship" and waited expectantly. The *kapitan* seemed to falter for a moment, and then filling the office with the sweetest music this side of heaven went on to answer in a wrenched rendition of the English language. We exchanged smiles. I switched to English.

With that subtle shift in mood, the house of cards I had been assembling began to tumble; the steam went out of the defection pitch. I asked the question I had to: "Why do you want a transit visa for the United States?" The *kapitan*'s answer was to the point. It was imperative that he return to the Soviet Union immediately, a family emergency, and he had found out that the quickest way to do so was by air via the United States. It was that simple. I looked into his eyes and knew he was telling the truth.

I called in a visa section clerk and explained that the man should be issued the transit visa at once. I shook the *kapitan*'s hand and left. End of operation, but the beginning of doubts about the defector-inducement program of the Soviet division.

7

OPERATION OX:
Counterintelligence Bungling

MUCH of the titillating flavor to an operation against two mysterious and elusive Soviets stems from my principal agent in the case. It was the agent who contributed the name to the operation, "the Ox," a name I could not help but use from the beginning, after debriefing the agent, and the only term that conveys the ironies underlying the operation.

The case began when I received a call from an eager collaborator, the naval attaché of the embassy. He had a visitor in his office telling a wild tale of some Russians who were acting very suspiciously and whom he had overheard mentioning Guantanamo, cannon, and the like. Would I come down to his office and see what sense I could make out of the mess? I went, on the run.

When I entered the attaché's office, I was in for a shock. The visitor was a huge man who bulged up and out of his chair as if he were perched on a stool. Above the bulk and the thick neck of a wrestler was a chubby, florid face with geniality written all over it. We were introduced. The informant began to repeat the essentials of the story he had told the attaché, the latter nodding confirmation. As he proceeded, growing more excited in the telling, I found myself only half listening. Something was pushing into my brain for attention, spreading over obstacles like a lava flow, gathering force. A few days earlier, I remembered, I had gone to the communications office to see a particular item of special intelligence*, making

---

*Communications intelligence.

a routine mental note of its contents. To the best of my recollection it had read: "TWO RUSSIANS (their names were given) OF THE (innocuous-sounding, perhaps Metallurgical or some such) DIRECTORATE (of the appropriate Ministry) HAVE DEPARTED FOR CUBA." It was a routine travel notification.

But as the Ox was talking in the naval attaché's office, the item limned up in my memory and seemed to be wanting to tell me something. It suddenly flashed to me: That innocuous-sounding directorate was a Soviet cover name for the chief armaments directorate of heavy industry. That knowledge was a flashback to my pre-CIA period when I was working in the National Security Agency. Of all the case officers in the Clandestine Services, it was I by extraordinary coincidence who could have provided the missing link that coupled the Ox's Russians to the Soviet armament experts.

Beyond that, the key phrases and words that were overheard suggested that the Soviet arms officials had surveyed the situation around the Guantanamo Naval Base in Oriente Province, including a possibility of ringing it with either defensive or offensive weapons, or both. That line of speculation, in turn, could have almost breakthrough significance for the current estimate of the extent and intensity of Soviet commitment to the Cubans. In short, by my reckoning, we had by a lucky stroke latched on to highly important information.

I stopped the informant abruptly in his recital, giving every evidence, I am sure, of my own excitement. I thanked the naval attaché profusely for having brought this matter to my notice. I turned to the big man, who was struggling to emerge from his chair, and said, "Come on. Let's go somewhere where we can talk." Like a terrier badgering an elephant I hustled him through the door, leaving behind a very confused naval attaché.

We had a protracted lunch in one of Havana's most prestigious restaurants. During the ordering and eating of the meal up to coffee, high as I was over my discovery, I conversed casually with my ponderous companion, who exhibited an enormous appetite. Without reservation, he told me who he was, what he was doing in Cuba, [eighteen words deleted], how it was that he was fluent in Russian. In that connection, besides mentioning his [two words deleted], he cited the source from which I later learned the details about a person described there simply as "the Ox."

I do not divulge the documentary source from which the agent purported to prove that he was called the Ox, for I cannot be certain that he has left Cuba. The source, however, described the Ox as an organizer of Gestapo espionage in the Low Countries during the days of brutal hidden warfare between the goons of the Communist International and Hitler. It also told a gory story of how the Ox was slain one foggy night by Comintern agents, or at least how his ripped body pitched into the river and was carried away by the current.

The Ox assured me that the report of his death was highly exaggerated, as was the allegation that he had been an agent of the Gestapo.

Over coffee, he related his story of the Russians, striving to be accurate. A few nights before, the Ox was sitting alone in the semi-darkness of the main bar of the Hotel Habana Libre. He became aware of a conversation in Russian between two men sitting at the bar. By straining he was able to overhear most of what was being said. The two were talking about a trip to Oriente Province at the eastern end of Cuba. He caught the words "Guantanamo," "a ring around the base," "cannon," "armaments," "fire power," and the like. He heard them discuss a Russian ship carrying munitions for Cuba, which had run aground off northern Africa in the Mediterranean.

Then the men left the bar and moved into the lounge of the hotel, seating themselves in a small enclave where they were alone. The Ox followed, and got as close as he dared. He heard only incoherent bits of conversation, but took careful notice of their appearance.

I interrupted the Ox and asked for a complete physical description of the Russians, which I jotted in my notebook. Both men were dressed in sports clothes, slacks, open-neck shirts. Comrade A was a shade taller than Comrade B, although similar in physique, hefty but not fat. Their eyes appeared to be blue, but that was uncertain. Comrade A had an ample shock of black hair; Comrade B's, equally full, was brown. There were no outstanding physical features or distinguishing marks.

I concluded by asking the Ox to frequent the Habana Libre bar every evening, and made arrangements for meeting him daily thereafter. Impulsively, I dug into my pockets and thrust a fistful of Cuban pesos at him, without even thinking of asking for a receipt. I paid the restaurant bill and we parted.

I cabled the information in its entirety to Headquarters, including a reference to the source identifying the Ox (which I had looked into as soon as I returned to the station). With the whole story wrapped up and sent to Headquarters, I waited impatiently for reaction to it. Though I met the Ox daily thereafter, he had nothing to report. The Russians had dropped from sight. I fretted. I checked with communications to verify that the cable had been sent and received. I couldn't imagine what was holding up a cabled reply from Headquarters. Time was of the essence, if we were to launch an all-out effort, maximizing the assets of the station, to locate the Russians, who might be up to other shenanigans in the line of duty.

A nerve-racking week passed by. Then, the anticlimactic answer came, by pouch. The reply cast doubt on the identification of the Russians as the arms experts, because one of the named comrades about whom Headquarters had information was bald, and my account had both men with full heads of hair. Not a word about the aspects of their conversation that indicated (no matter who they were) that they were involved in some highly significant activity in Cuba.

I throttled my frustration, somewhat unstoically and ungracefully, but resolved at least to salvage what I could of the situation. I proposed to Headquarters that I recruit the Ox as an agent, citing his anti-communist attitude, his fluency in Russian, his ability to float around Havana without arousing suspicion, his usefulness at gatherings where Russians were in attendance. Pending clearance of the Ox, I kept him on the string and used him sparingly.

Then the other shoe dropped! Out of gratitude for his having provided the lead to the Ox, I had kept my colleague, the naval attaché, fairly well informed on early developments in the operation and its promise in matters military. When my phone rang and a secretary told me that the naval attaché was calling, I had an uncontrollable feeling that something was up about the Ox. Extrasensory perception, perhaps. He asked me to come to his office because he had just received a strange report from one of his informants. I rushed down, wild hopes reviving.

The naval attaché, who had not been aware of the stalemate in my case, told me quite casually the following story: "One of my boys has been keeping his eyes and ears open out at the Comodoro Hotel [a beachfront hotel known to be frequented for recreation purposes by Russians]. He's been seeing these same two Russians coming out of the hotel every day going to the pool for a swim. Then, one day he sees the same two guys, only something's different with one of them. One of the guys is completely bald. One day a full head of hair, and the next a shiny bald dome. What do you make of it?"

I could have kissed the naval attaché right then and there. But I asked, "When did your boy see the Russians?" He figured it to have taken place about a week and a half before, in other words, in a time frame during which the Ox also had seen the Russians. It fit. Not hiding my elation, I related the comedy (or tragedy) of errors to the attaché, patted him on the back, and asked him to contact his informant for more recent information on the same two Russians. I was planning to get the Ox out to the hotel as soon as possible to case the situation, to determine the whereabouts of the Russians, to locate their room number, to obtain their names from the hotel register. Despite the ironic twist that might have revived Headquarters' acceptance of the Russians as the arms experts, and my zeal to push forward, I had a feeling in my bones that it was too late. Nevertheless, I cabled the latest information to Headquarters.

The next day I received word from Headquarters, again by

pouch, and obviously a response to an earlier message. The dispatch made no reference to Operation Ox and the Russians, but issued a warning not to use the Ox operationally (a cut below outright refusal of clearance). The CI staff had checked the source given to me by the Ox and preferred to believe that the source account of the Ox was true, that he was a Gestapo agent, and that he was dead! Though I won't reveal the source, I thought it a rattling good collection of fairy tales. It was incomprehensible to me, however, that grown men in the counterintelligence business should swallow it whole.

The end came to Operation Ox when it was subsequently learned that the Russians had checked out of the Hotel Comodoro prior to the time of the naval attaché's story of the disappearing wig. If the whole episode provided any input to the Agency's estimate of Russian commitment or intentions toward Cuba, I never heard of it.

The processes of intelligence collection I have just described were those peculiar to Cuba at the time. But the inadequacies, imperfections, and frustrations, for the three forms of intelligence collection I dealt with (counterintelligence, positive intelligence, and operational intelligence), are shortcomings exemplary of the workings of classic espionage within the framework of the modern clandestine intelligence bureaucracy.

Classic espionage is the bread-and-butter activity of the CIA's field stations. Those who are engaged in the time-honored profession tend to coast along on the assumption that what is collected by secret means is inherently worthwhile. Yet in my first sustained endeavors as a spy, it became increasingly apparent that the accomplishment fell far short of the expectation.

Though some of the preceding operations must by professional standards be accounted failures, there was fallout from them of more than passing influence for me. Even as a case officer devoted to the missions of the Agency, my views altered due to circumstance. My earliest experiences in Cuba, for example, taught me the absurdity of labeling Castro and his regime as communist and the people of Cuba as brain-washed revolutionaries. In like manner, my first closer associations with Russians, even within an operational framework, revealed how unlike the communist stereotype they were. Once I began to squirm from beneath the ideological stranglehold of the Clandestine Services, with its fixation on deadly warfare against the communist "forces of evil," the path toward realistically assessing the nature of the intelligence game I was playing became clearer.

8

PLANTING BUGS:
The Search for the Soviet Embassy-To-Be

WITHOUT question the dominant concern of the Soviet division was to discover where the Soviets were going to locate their embassy in Havana. The pressure was on to find the chosen site as quickly as possible, allowing lead time for an entry operation to place electronic bugs, preferably in the ambassador's office. It was reasonable to expect that Aleksandr, the *Rezident*, was also under pressure to scout out a suitable embassy location.

If only it had been Aleksandr alone that we had to worry about. The search for the Soviet Embassy site was becoming the hottest topic of conversation in Havana, not only on the cocktail circuit but also in the *cafecito* stalls at every street corner in town. I take as gospel what *Habaneros* proclaim — that Havana is the rumor mill capital of the world. Wherever two people congregate, their union seems to give birth to a new rumor. Reports came pouring in to the station, citing first one place that the Soviets had selected, then another, all with superficially convincing evidence.

If the RIS had deliberately floated the rumors, it couldn't have devised a better stratagem to confuse the enemy. The case officer is duty bound to pass judgment on each and every rumor. He makes his lists, watching for repeats, crosschecking evidence, and pressuring agents through their case officers to amplify or certify the information. Many hours were spent inside the station in this form of intelligence analysis. Outside, I felt compelled to check every site, putting myself in the place of Aleksandr to judge the criteria that would presumably appeal to the Russians. I hung around so many places that if Cuban G-2 or the Havana police were suspicious of me or had had any reason to sack me, they could have legitimately picked me up for loitering a dozen times.

There was no letup in the furious pace of the rumors. The Soviets, of course, were now the fair-haired boys in Cuba, and it could be conjectured that they would select an imposing and spacious site to demonstrate to the world not only their solidarity with the Cubans but also the seriousness of their intentions to befriend a communist-leaning ally. On the grounds of grandeur alone, it was possible to discard some of the rumors that would have put the Soviet Embassy into less prestigious accommodations. All the more credible targets were dutifully reported to Headquarters.

Most of the reports were coming from agents of my case officer colleagues who knew Havana much better than I. So, from our continuing discussions, I fell in with a consensus that seemed to be forming around one particular site. The more the one stood over the others, the more certain we were that we had discovered the Soviets' choice. Of course, I could not convey such certainty to Headquarters, but simply laid out the mounting evidence that seemed to point in one direction. I included accompanying rumors that indicated an early occupancy by the Soviets. I must have struck a nerve. The response from Headquarters was swift and unequivocal: get cracking, penetrate the target and install listening devices.

Operation Rosita

Had there been no rumors, and had I put myself in the place of Aleksandr to select the best possible site for the Soviet Embassy (as I did mentally when casing some of the earlier-rumored sites), I would have chosen the Hotel Rosita de Hornedo anyway. It had everything going for it. One of the newer hotels in Havana, regarded as just a shade less pretentious than the Hotel Nacional and lacking the glamor of the group of "tourist" showplaces like the Hotels Riviera, Capri, and Hilton, the Hotel Rosita (as it was called) probably best represented modern Cuban taste. Though it had been built by one of the oldest and richest families of Cuba, the Soviets may well have been inclined to overlook its capitalist credentials because rumors were flying thick and fast that it was about to be "intervened" by Castro (a fancy word for seizure by the state).

The hotel was situated just outside the hub district of Havana across the Almendares River, with easy access by bridge or tunnel to the city. It occupied a relatively isolated spot of the Miramar beach area, with the sea directly at its back. It was of sufficient size that if the Soviets were merely to occupy a few floors as offices, they could set up a first-rate installation and still have living quarters in the hotel for all. Its crowning glory was a vast, richly furnished room at the top, with massive picture windows facing the sea, and, Soviet delight, access to it could be easily controlled. That penthouse room was made to order for the ambassador's office.

In general, electronic eavesdropping usually requires the calling in of Agency technicians for the precarious work of installing the tap or bug. (The technicians know full well that they are violating the laws of a foreign country.) An agent must be located in a nearby "listening post" to monitor, replenish reels, and record the transmissions emitted from the source instruments. The pattern of operational flow is then in place: to recover tapes from the agent; to have them translated into English; to have them screened locally for technical performance and evidence of "compromise" (operational intelligence). Positive intelligence will be extracted and reported to Headquarters. With so many links in the chain of the operation, overall security is often put to a strain.

The first step in "getting cracking" was to case the situation at the Hotel Rosita thoroughly. It was not a one-man or one-man-and-secretary job, but required a generous assist from the station. One case officer turned over to me for my exclusive use one of his best agents – a young man who knew Havana inside and out and perhaps more important, knew the people who knew most about the Hotel Rosita de Hornedo.

Operation Rosita would not have come to fruition without that young man, whom I shall call Armando. (I still remember him with affection, and pray that he survived the Bay of Pigs invasion and its aftermath, or made his escape from Cuba.) The chief of station was acquainted with a foreign ambassador who was living in the hotel, and arranged for me to have a confidential interview with him.

By such measures, combined with personal visits to the hotel and its environs, I was able to compile a creditable casing report covering personnel, hotel routine, physical layout and security. During the investigation, new evidence of Soviet interest in the hotel was introduced, which only whetted Headquarters' appetite for getting along with the next, more ticklish part of the operation — penetration of the hotel and installation of the bugs.

Thus before long, the experts — two technicians of the Technical Services division of the Clandestine Services — were dispatched to Havana. They arrived as ordinary tourists, with just their personal belongings. Many of the tools of their trade were on hand, stored in the station, and whatever else they needed would be sent by pouch. One of the technicians was an old hand; his assistant was on his first foreign assignment. They put up at one of the hotels near the American Embassy, but very prudently never put in an appearance at the embassy during daylight working hours.

When we met to discuss the operation, sometimes during nocturnal visits to the embassy to check the gear, I learned what it meant to be the case officer for an operation of this nature. If I thought (as I did in my ignorance) that I would be only tailing along, I was very much mistaken. I was in charge; it was my operation; it was my responsibility not only to support it to the hilt but to lead the way with respect to the security measures required for the technicians' safety. The technicians were entirely correct in making those points clear; their expertise was technical; mine was in clandestine technique. There was no denying it; it was their skin. In effect, they were my agents, and it is the agent who runs the risks and gets it in the neck if caught.

Nothing was left to chance in planning the operation. Armando was brought into the thick of it, not only for his extensive knowledge of the Hotel Rosita, but also for his raw courage and his willingness amounting to eagerness to perform along with the technicians. As if that were not enough, it turned out that Armando lived in a building that was [six words deleted] to set up a listening post, a crucial part of the operation. Several sessions were devoted to a paper exercise of what was going to take place, down to the minutest detail.

The plan was to place a microphone-transmitter in the ceiling of the penthouse room expected to be occupied by the Soviet ambassador. If not used for the ambassador, the room still was the ideal spot for holding meetings and discussions, or in any event would likely be reserved for the top people of the embassy, not excluding the KGB complement. Entry of the room would take place toward midnight, when fewest personnel were active about the hotel. The elevators to the penthouse were to be checked out beforehand by Armando, who at the same time would map out the route of access to the penthouse proper and take impressions of the locks of entry doors. An eyewitness account of the interior and furnishings of the big room at the top permitted calculations to be made of how the ceiling could be reached, the kind of plaster and material that would be needed to restore its original appearance after the bug had been planted, and most important, what escape routes were available in case the technicians were interrupted at work. Armando was to remain on guard in the room with a walkie-talkie while the technicians were attaching the transmitter.

There was a major security hurdle to overcome prior to and during the installation, to get the two technicians and Armando into the hotel with their gear, up to the penthouse area, and to establish a lookout point. The problem was settled in a remarkably simple manner, by throwing an honest-to-goodness ripsnorting party at the hotel the night of the entry. We had a winsome young secretary of the station rent a suite of rooms close to an elevator. She unabashedly stated her purpose when reserving the suite, and won the approving assent of the hotel clerk. We invited a congenial mix of bachelors and single girls of the station, and briefed them on the part they were to play in the forthcoming operation. They vowed they would make it a party to remember and have it going full blast by the time the technicians, Armando, and I arrived carrying more "goodies" to the festivities. I would remain behind at the party to work the walkie-talkie and maintain the lookout when the others took off.

The night of the party was right out of a Cuban travel folder, with balmy breezes playing over sand and sea, and a bright moon sending a shaft of shimmering light along the water to the beach at the base of the Hotel Rosita, whose upper reaches were bathed by that same moon in an eerie greenish glow. The moonlight etched four silent figures as they stole forth from the American Embassy lugging their gaily wrapped pieces of gear. The party was in full swing when we arrived. We joined in, drinking a round or two to be sociable, dancing perfunctorily now and then, mostly beating time to the music from the record player just to show that our spirits were up, until the moment of truth.

At a sign from one of the young men that the elevator was ready at the floor and that the coast was clear, Armando and the technicians slipped out the open door and in an instant were swallowed up by the elevator. It had been agreed that Armando would contact me by walkie-talkie as soon as they made entry to the penthouse. We waited what seemed an interminable time, losing any stomach for even the pretense of partying; all eyes were fixed on the walkie-talkie I was holding to my ear. Then the voice came, low but clear, a simple O.K. Drinks were poured, glasses touched, and the party went on.

An hour and a half at the outside had been scheduled for the installation, taking the operation well past midnight. Just before returning, Armando was to send me a signal, to which I would respond with the "all clear." The hour and a half came and went. I alone knew the schedule and began to grow very apprehensive. My imagination began playing all kinds of tricks. I distinctly recall worrying whether our game plan called for drawing the curtains of the picture window if the moon were shining in. Finally a hardly audible crackle came from the walkie-talkie – I looked in panic to see whether "Receive" was on, and then I heard the words, "We're ready."

In moments the three agents returned, their mission successfully accomplished, to a much relieved case officer and to a tumultuous welcome from the others. We four were the first to leave, driving with all our gear over to Armando's apartment, from which the next phase of the operation was to be handled.

Armando's apartment, [three words deleted], occupied the [six words deleted]. We conducted our test experiments on the roof over several nights to determine whether the Rosita bug was in good working order and to register the best frequency fix on it. It was a weird sight: We sat transfixed or moved about like voiceless zombies in the gloom of night. Two of us sat with padded phones over our ears, twirling the dials of the receivers to the required frequency to catch the slightest evidence of sound from the darkened room of the Hotel Rosita. When we heard a discernible source of sound, we silently handed over our headphones to the other two. We were actors in slow motion on a darkened soundless stage. But once, while we huddled over the apparatus, the lights went on in the penthouse! We listened intently and let out muffled cheers: We could hear what was going on in that room as plain as day, even the wisecracks in Spanish as some servants went about dusting the furniture.

Satisfied that we had a good listening post, we set up the receiving equipment in Armando's apartment in a second bedroom. Armando, who was [one word deleted], assured us that *that* bedroom would not be used, since he had his lady friends over only one at a time. We arranged an interim monitoring schedule with Armando which, naturally, would be tailored to different requirements once the Soviets were in.

The technicians, who had grown to appreciate the admirable qualities of their Cuban colleague, took their sad farewells of Armando. I said my equally sad good-byes to the technicians, because we had become fast friends under very trying conditions, working feverishly to get the job done before the

Soviets beat us to the punch.

By this time I had moved from my room at the Hotel Capri in downtown Havana to a private home in the ritzy suburb of Marianao. Although I was farther removed from the scene of action, it didn't matter that much: With the basics for Operation Rosita in place waiting to be activated only when the Russians moved in, I had little need to keep Armando abreast of day-to-day developments. For my part, however, stimulated by pressures from Headquarters, I was immersed in what amounted to a pseudo-scientific guessing game about the move-in date for the Russians. As time passed and predicted dates did not materialize, I lost my ardor. I and others concerned in the operation simply shrugged off concern about the date, taking comfort in our certainty of Russian occupation of the Rosita and the fact that it was only a matter of time. Armando, for all I knew, might have found a more immediate use for the second bedroom.

Then, the fairy's wand descended, bringing its ironic reward to all our efforts. It was a Saturday morning, and I was still lounging around in my pajamas after an uncommonly fine breakfast prepared by the cook (who came with the house). There was a knock at the door. Still clutching my morning newspaper, I opened the door to a Cuban gentleman who stood with a very puzzled look on his face. He was holding an official-looking piece of paper in his hand. Waving the paper, he asked me in Spanish, "Is this the address for the Soviet Embassy?"

Stunned into doing exactly the right thing, I gave no answer but mechanically removed the paper from the Cuban's hand. He went on to explain that he was an electrician and had an order to check the wiring of the Soviet Embassy, and pointing to the sheet in my hand, he asked again if this house was the address written on the sheet. I looked at the work-order: unquestionably official, issued by some Cuban Ministry or other; *Embajada Sovietica* in bold face upper-case type; and below it the address in the suburb of Marianao. I handed back the work-order to the electrician and said, "*Señor*, you are just one block away from the Soviet Embassy." I pointed across the way to the rear of an unoccupied mansion that fronted its iron gates on the next street, whose address carried a five-digit number quite close to mine.

Wings of victory could not have propelled me any faster than I made it to the station that Saturday morning. I rushed in to the communications office and begged the officer to send the following urgent message: "KNOW FOR CERTAIN REPEAT CERTAIN WHERE SOVIET EMBASSY TO BE LOCATED."

Only later that day did I realize that I never told Headquarters that my certainty ruled out the Hotel Rosita de Hornedo. I was so consumed with the miracle — I, of the countless thousands in Havana, was the one to whom the divine truth was revealed — that I shed not one tear over the Hotel Rosita or even cared that it now was too late to try to bug the Soviet Embassy. For the remainder of my stay in Cuba, I got a kick out of watching the Cuban crews sprucing up my neighbor's home.

Still, I must draw the moral from all this, especially since the guilt was mine. Although I had made a few observations that indicated a glaring disparity between operational goals and results, I had become an uncomplaining and uncritical participant in that crushing compulsion to reach the goal, to get the job done. Inescapably, the deeper one gets into the job, the more one's assets and energies are committed, the more absorbed one becomes in the mechanics of clandestinity, the less attention one gives to prudent assessment or common sense caution. Thus, with Operation Rosita there need not have been that imperative to "get cracking." Possibly, if I had been a more seasoned operator, I might have urged caution about going out on a limb — but I wasn't and I didn't. And later there were indeed occasions when a proposed operation looked like utter foolishness to me but I went ahead and complied anyway.

In intelligence work, the proclivity toward concentration on technical or methodological aspects of an operation to the virtual dismissal or exclusion of other factors is called "operations for operations' sake." Call it a proclivity, a state of mind, the clandestine mentality or simply shortsightedness, operations for operations' sake were benignly tolerated throughout the Clandestine Services, not just in the Soviet division, and extended to every conceivable class: espionage, counterintelligence or political/paramilitary action.

Whether or not one can as a practical matter do anything to diminish "operations for operations' sake," one must call attention to the ease with which intelligence agencies slide into the practice.

9

THE RELUCTANT STUDENT OPERATION:
An Innocent Abroad?

MUCH as I was absorbed in counterintelligence work against the Russians, I still hankered for a good old-fashioned espionage operation that would produce information about Russia itself. But I had given little thought to how it would be handled in a country hostile to the United States.

When normal relations exist between the United States and a host country, a positive intelligence operation, the purpose of which is to collect information from or about the Soviet Union, may develop in a number of ways. The most prolific source of "leads" to prospective travelers to and from the Soviet Union is a local travel agency. It is with good reason that intelligence training manuals and courses stress the value of seeking recruitments, almost as standard operating procedure, among travel agencies. In earlier days at least, especially with respect to the Soviets, it was a "must" for case officers to attempt recruitments at the limited number of local agencies to whom Soviet travel had been entrusted by INTURIST, the Soviet Travel Agency. Once accomplished, however, the recruitment tended to be long-lasting, even though — and this is an example of the gamesmanship between intelligence professionals — the Soviets probably knew that "their" agency had been penetrated by the opposition. The byplay aside, a case officer could rely on "his" travel agency to furnish advance information on prospective travel to or from the Soviet Union. Occasionally, lead material came from more "sensitive" files at Headquarters. And lastly, locals contemplating a trip to the Soviet Union might "walk in" to the American Embassy to declare their intentions, usually out of fear of jeopardizing their travel permits to the United States.

In the latter case, more often than not, the "declarer" (referred, of course, to a case officer) might be easily prevailed upon to perform a few services for the United States. In the greater number of cases, however, by screening the leads supplied by travel agencies, running traces at Headquarters, and conducting local investigations, the case officer could brief himself well before deciding how he would go about making the pitch to his prospective agent. The implied weight of official United States purpose was ordinarily sufficient to achieve a high batting average of recruitments. With his agent on the string, the case officer buckled down to the serious job of providing him with the "requirements" of his mission, tailored naturally to the traveler's itinerary and freedom of movement. The traveler was carefully briefed in the art of observation, techniques for "innocent" recording of his observations, and gimmicks for verifying detail and measurement. After a security briefing on the pitfalls and snares the traveler could expect from the omnipresent RIS (the traveler was cautioned to regard every INTURIST guide as an RIS agent), the traveler was slapped on the back and sent on his way, instructed to report to the case officer for debriefing as soon as he returned.

A break for which I was continually on the lookout fell into my lap one day when a young Cuban man, apparently fearful of having been selected to undergo training in the Soviet Union, landed at my desk. It's not quite accurate to say "my" desk because when the young man, whom I shall call Aurelio, met me for the first time, it was at a desk in the cultural attaché's office, plainly posted as such along with the name of the attaché. It was a standard precaution in a case of this type to pose as an embassy officer, for if the student were a plant by the opposition intelligence service, we would want to reduce the damages to the CIA to a minimum.

Aurelio's tangled story revealed that he was just a simple

soldier of Raul Castro's armed forces. He had no idea why he had been chosen for higher training at a military school in the Soviet Union. He said he was not a political person, although he confessed an antipathy toward communism and the Russians. He was at a loss to explain why Fidel Castro's revolution, which he had supported, was becoming involved with the Russians. Also, he said he was frightened about leaving his family and Cuba for parts unknown.

So far, so good, especially that last part of being frightened to undertake the mission. It didn't seem as if he were acting under instructions to bestir CIA interest in him. But maybe he was really a pretty cool customer, a sophisticated operative in his own right. So I decided to keep playing it straight.

I asked the young soldier, who certainly backed up that part of his story by appearing in his casual uniform, what he thought the American Embassy could do about his plight. Aurelio seemed to be flustered by the question; his face fell. He began again to recite his story of his humble station in life, his hatred of communism, and his fear of being forced to go to the Soviet Union. I commiserated with him, but asked again why he had come to the American Embassy with his troubles.

At that, Aurelio became genuinely distressed. He stood up, rubbed his hands together, took a step away from his chair, returned and sat down. A simple fellow, agitated, confused? I didn't know, so I tried a different tack. I asked a series of questions about his life: birth date, place of birth, family and relatives, schooling and such, to keep him talking.

At the conclusion of this line of questioning, he was still fidgeting. Heaving a mock sigh of resignation, I told Aurelio that, regretfully, if he had no request of the embassy, there was nothing I could see that the American Embassy could do for him. Almost in a panic he blurted out, "Let me talk with the CIA." Without batting an eye, I replied that I would report his case to the CIA, and asked him for a telephone number where he could be reached. Without answering, he bolted from his chair and fled. End of scene. We never heard from him or of him again.

The Operation of the Reluctant Student was not much of

an operation, at least on our part. The uncertainties and frustrations encountered in my conversation with Aurelio were certainly compounded by my lack of competence in speaking Spanish and his difficulty with English. Woe to the case officer, even one with non-native fluency in the language of the agent, who fails to recognize that his pitch for recruitment, his instructing and debriefing the agent, are very shaky indeed. Even good operations can falter on these grounds.

But from the telltale outburst about the CIA, the appearance of Aurelio at the embassy had all the earmarks of a Cuban penetration operation, designed probably to encourage the CIA to run the student in the U.S.S.R., or more modestly, to pinpoint CIA officers in the embassy.

I would have loved to have been eavesdropping when Aurelio reported back to his superiors. He may have had a hard time describing to G-2 the line of questioning he had faced from the "cultural attaché."

10

COMMUNICATIONS INTELLIGENCE:
The Cuban Codebook

NOWADAYS, "communications intelligence" has become almost a household phrase. The syndicated columnist Jack Anderson often refers to it and even describes (in fairly accurate detail) the most "sensitive" of communications operations. I am not qualified to describe the technical deployment and expertise of the National Security Agency's communications operations or its developments of cryptographic methodology. Nor is it my purpose to wander into the equally fascinating area, more within the ken of the CIA, to be found in the secret communications of clandestine agents. I shall state my opinions, though, of NSA's product, which in the intelligence trade is known as special intelligence (SI).

From my service in NSA I gained an insider's appreciation for the values and limitations of special intelligence. Indeed, it was because of my familiarity with communications intelligence that I was recruited by the CIA for assignment to the Soviet division of the Clandestine Services. Once aboard, I was able to gauge pretty well how the Agency measured up in its exploitation of special intelligence. On the "overt" analytical side of the Agency, I found that much progress had been made with the relatively new (to them) source, both in learning the tricks of the trade and discovering the ways in which the SI contribution could be maximized.

The first lesson that the CIA absorbed about special intelligence was that it perished if it was allowed to fall on barren soil. The analysts had perceived the necessity of being extraordinarily well-versed in their particular areas of knowledge, whether of politics, economic resources, or nuts and bolts. Without that base, the capacity of SI to add to that knowledge in specificity and unique detail could easily slip by. The outstanding characteristic of SI was its reliability, thus underpinning the entire structure of knowledge built by the analysts, and perhaps more importantly providing the vital ingredient of confirmation to information already assembled. In the intelligence reporting business, reliability of the information is the name of the game.

On the clandestine side of the house, with its emphasis on operations, I found that special intelligence had only the most limited application. It served no key purpose of confirming anything operational. In fact, it was considered a hindrance by "operators" who dislike strictures imposed by the sensitivity of the source on their free-wheeling course of action. However, it did provide isolated instances of assistance to operational matters. For the "legal travel" program it occasionally identified persons who would be traveling either to or from the Soviet Union, and often carried a built-in advantage of providing lead time for operational development.

The major flaw in the CIA's utilization of special intelligence, as I saw it, was the CIA's exaggerated sense of security consciousness about the source. Long after the other countries of the world, even the smallest and poorest, had grown sophisticated in their knowledge of communications intelligence reality, the major intelligence agencies of the United States continued to regard special intelligence in a sacred light. Possibly the glow lingered from the time of World War II, when the codeword "Magic" was used to describe code-breaking successes against the enemy. No doubt NSA's parental concern for its brainchild was impressed on user agencies. In clearance procedures for users within the CIA, the tale was solemnly told of the prominent person who during World War II was suffered to go to his death in a plane shot down by the enemy, rather than to have revealed our "compromise" of the enemy's code. At any rate, the practical results from the cult worship were that only limited numbers of analysts and operational personnel were cleared to use SI materials, and in subtle ways the more productive use of the source was inhibited.

So pervasive was the aura of sanctity that attached to special intelligence that the agency that produced it and the agencies that used it often seemed to be procedurally prostrate before it (frightened to death that something might fall into the hands of the "enemy" and give the show away). There is a fine example of such behavior in my own experience, although my evidence is purely circumstantial.

One day in June 1960 I left my room in the Hotel Capri in Havana and entered the self-service elevator. To my surprise there were two other Americans in the elevator, young men, dressed in fairly sloppy sports outfits. Americans in Havana were rare in those days, but I was most struck by the aloofness of the two, who gave no sign of their recognition of a fellow American. I shrugged off this queer behavior on their part and promptly forgot the whole incident. Later I learned that two employees of the National Security Agency, Bernon Mitchell and William H. Martin, defected to Russia in June 1960. The reports of their escape route took them to Havana, Cuba, from where they boarded a Russian ship sailing to the Soviet Union. As I reconstructed the affair, I concluded that the day I saw those two young men in the elevator coincided with the day they must have been in Cuba. Imagine my chagrin. I could have been a hero. As a cleared SI officer in Havana, I might have been alerted by NSA (through CIA) that two men had defected from NSA and *might* be fleeing the country (Cuba, at the time, was a promising escape route or haven). Warned in time to maintain a lookout, when the golden opportunity arrived I might have marshaled the considerable resources of the United States Embassy in Havana, including the FBI, to effect a capture of the two escapees. As it is, it will always remain a tantalizing memory of the good old days.*

The mystique surrounding communications intelligence,

---

*(Publisher's Note) The author was unaware at the time of writing this book that the National Security Agency had *not*, according to James Bamford's *The Puzzle Palace* (p. 141), discovered Mitchell's and Martin's flight on June 25, 1960 until more than a month later, because they were supposedly on vacation.

ascribing almost magic qualities to the source, prompted CIA operations that suffered from the same myopia of "operations for operations' sake" that affects propaganda, deception, and other communications-related operations. The classic example is the "Berlin Tunnel" operation, which was widely publicized as an intelligence coup. As a technical operation it was a latter-day miracle, down to the beefed-up air conditioning system to prevent the snows overhead in East German territory from melting and revealing the tunnel beneath. The tap on the communications nexus of the Soviet forces in East Germany was an engineering marvel. Others, including the communists themselves, have paid due tribute to the tunnel's ingenuity and magnitude.

But what of the intelligence "take" from so imaginative and costly a venture? I regret to say that apart from some up-to-date "order of battle" on Soviet and East German military outfits (as if it mattered), the massive outpouring of information from the operation was embarrassingly insignificant in substance. Yet a sizable task force of translators (of whom I was one) labored for months in hush-hush surroundings to produce what was essentially low-level information that a hustling agent or two might have collected. When it was all over, the Director personally thanked the task force for their efforts in a job splendidly done. In retrospect, it was one of those grandiose operations that should never have got off the ground, no pun intended.

I should explain that I consider communications intelligence probably the most misunderstood of all forms of intelligence. I do not refer to misunderstanding by the analysts who use it, but to the overseers of the intelligence establishment, and that reaches high into government. The fuzziness about "communications intelligence" has crept upward into the councils of those who draw the parameters of and define the country's "national security."

I am indebted to Jack Anderson for revealing in the spring of 1974 circumstances that bear out the substance of my allegation. Some three years before, Anderson published a story about CIA eavesdropping on the telephone traffic between the limousines of Kremlin leaders. At that time he wrote, "for years the CIA has been able to listen to the kingpins of the Kremlin banter, bicker and backbite among themselves." A CIA source confirmed to him at the time that Soviet leaders did not hold strategy sessions in their limousines, but that the "small talk" did provide insight into their personalities. The CIA source said the transcripts also showed that the Kremlin chiefs were aware that they were being overheard. Not long afterward, the so-called "plumbers unit" set up in the Nixon White House to investigate "leaks" began checking into Anderson's account of the Kremlin bugging. Alarmed, then CIA Director Richard Helms talked to Anderson, asked him not to mention the eavesdropping operation in his forthcoming book, acknowledged that the Kremlin leaders knew their conversations had been monitored, and urged Anderson never to mention how the conversations were intercepted. In the 1974 column, Anderson summed up his belief that the White House seized on the "plumbers" investigation of the Anderson "leaks" to clothe the independent White House operators in the mantle of "national security." His rebuttal to that claim was: the monitored Kremlin chitchat was never an important intelligence source; his earlier story revealed nothing the Kremlin leaders didn't already know; and consequently "the President's claim of national security simply won't wash."

It's not often in the shadowy world of "spooks and spies" that one finds as clear a statement as the above of the "realities" of intelligence. Such candor in the realm of communications intelligence is rare. Perhaps the foregoing may dispel to a degree the ignorance and misunderstanding caused by the excess of security and secrecy surrounding special intelligence.

Operation Codebook

Without a doubt the most highly revered prize of all intelligence effort is the "capture" of a codebook or cipher system of a current "enemy," especially without the enemy's knowledge that it has been compromised. In its innermost recesses, the Clandestine Services has a special staff responsible for the processing and handling of communications intelligence, including a super-secret component whose sole aim in life is to acquire foreign codes and ciphers by clandestine means. By some lucky chance, I was converted into a clandestine means toward that end.

A young Cuban who had just returned from his assignment at an overseas embassy had let it be known to someone in the American Embassy that he was willing to cooperate with Americans if they would guarantee his safe transit to the United States, and a hot potato like that fell to the station and somehow landed in my in-basket. The situation was a little off the beaten track for me, primarily because it involved a high order of personal security for the young diplomat, whom I shall call Ricardo.

In operating against the Russians in Cuba, I felt that my earlier conclusion was confirmed, that security demands for conducting such operations were highly overrated. While I maintained reasonable security in my work and was not prone to flout security simply because I believed that it unduly hampered operational work, I seldom drew in the reins because of what were conventionally assessed as high-risk situations. Those nocturnal meetings in the embassy with the technicians or our ghostly rooftop antics under a full moon raised no goosepimples. I had even less concern about myself when acting alone as an agent, because of my conviction that if the opposition really gave a damn about me there should have been some evidence to that effect.

But I could not adopt quite that cavalier an attitude toward Ricardo. He was, after all, one of theirs, a trusted official who had spent a tour in a Cuban embassy. He was privy to the acts and policies of the Castro administration toward other nations. And, as was expected and as I was soon to find out, he knew the Cuban diplomatic code. In short, he fit in very neatly with my theory that security for communist governments was mainly reserved for their own nationals. Following that dictum, it could not be ruled out that Cuban Army Military Intelligence (G-2) might be inclined to keep a watchful eye on a returned diplomat like Ricardo.

Our first meeting, carefully arranged through recognition signals, took place one dreary, dark night at the foot of the Maine Monument along the Malecón, Havana's sea-wall. We fenced our introductions, each intent on probing the other to take his measure, oblivious of the clouds of spray that swept in from the sea. Ricardo, I discovered, would play his chips of information and knowledge cautiously until such time as he had a binding agreement for getting him out of Cuba and re-settled in the United States. Realizing that his tactic might produce prolonged negotiations and an extended series of meetings, I suggested that our subsequent meetings take place in a safe house, to be divulged to Ricardo after our next encounter at the Maine Monument.

As case officer for an operation of this nature, I had to assume that it might be a plant, a means of legitimately moving a Cuban agent into the United States. There were no traces on Ricardo from Headquarters, except for the fact that he had been, as he said, stationed at a Cuban embassy. That meant that whether he were clean would have to be determined through perceptive assessment by the case officer and our evaluation of the worth of his information. (The use of a polygraph test is usually not entertained until much later in an operation, and then only because there may be a concrete reason to suspect the agent.)

My personal assessment of Ricardo, from our first meeting, was favorable: He appeared business-like, aware that he had something of value to impart for value received; he did not indulge in anti-Castro heroics; he seemed convincingly set on what he wanted his future to be and where he wanted it — in the United States, not in Cuba; and he had a healthy, realistic fear of the risks he was running. At our second meeting, I narrowed down the terms along which we would proceed: Ricardo to divulge the Cuban code; I to obtain Headquarters' agreement to his resettlement. I disclosed to him the building in which the apartment which served as a safe house was located, and worked out the schedule and security routine that would govern our future meetings.

The tricky part of the operation resulted from pacing the degree of assent to Ricardo's relocation in the United States to the amount and value of the information Ricardo would furnish. I entreated Headquarters to hasten its commitment to Ricardo, stressing the humanitarian aspect of dealing forthrightly and squarely with a person who was risking his life in associating with the Agency. The replies from Headquarters were equivocal, intimating that before they could go into high gear, there had to be proof positive of the value of Ricardo's information.

The first several sessions with Ricardo in the safe house, under the rules we had set, were not easy. I collected some low-level information about the life of a Cuban diplomat, the relations of Cuba with the country to which Ricardo had been accredited, and a smattering of other details about the Castro regime of which Ricardo had personal knowledge. Finally, I cut through the ambiguities from Headquarters that I had been feeding him and laid it on the line that Headquarters was not likely to move on his request for asylum until he had given us the Cuban code and Headquarters had checked out its authenticity.

The charade was over. Ricardo had been driven to the wall. In another session or two, he spelled out the coding system that had been in use for the Cuban Foreign Office and his embassy. It was a simple system that made use of the pagination and word order of a particular dictionary held in common by the Foreign Office and the embassy. Ricardo recalled that the same system was employed between embassies. He gave us a copy of the dictionary, which was little known and out of print.

I wish I could record that the operation came to a happy conclusion, after Ricardo had fulfilled his part of the bargain. Indeed, it was with great satisfaction both in Ricardo's performance and in mine for having captured such a prize that I sent off the complete wrap-up on the Cuban code to Headquarters. I urged rapid action because every day that Ricardo remained in Cuba presented danger for him.

Ricardo and I kept up our meetings, each one becoming drearier as we went along. I had nothing to tell him of Headquarters' plans; I had no stomach for further debriefing. Ricardo became visibly more dejected, and more apprehensive of the risks he was taking in meeting me. We consumed a lot of liquor in those meetings. The operation went downhill for about two weeks, including those last meetings, and then it was terminated by my sudden departure from Cuba, without even the opportunity to arrange for a turnover to another case officer.

Upon my return to Headquarters, I tried persistently to find out what had happened to Ricardo. But no answers were forthcoming. And what of the codebook? A wall of compartmentalization within the SI staff prevented me from even broaching the question. It was as though Operation Codebook had never taken place! I could swallow the omission of any recognition of me for having accomplished a significant mission, but I could not then, and have not to this day, reconciled myself to the probability that Ricardo was conveniently forgotten.

From left to right: Osvaldo Dorticós, Anastas Mikoyan, Fidel Castro, Carlos Rafael Rodríguez, and Raúl Castro, at José Martí International Airport, Havana, February 1960.

Soviet Scientific, Technical, and Cultural Exposition, Havana, February 1960, infiltrated by the author.

Model of Sputnik exhibited at Soviet Exposition, Havana, February 1960.

Mikoyan, Castro, and Dorticós pose after Soviet Exposition press conference at which the author found himself in the front row.

Left: The author and his wife, Judith, at the Hotel Capri, Havana, 1960. Right: The U.S. Embassy in Havana where the CIA station was located and the author's operations planned.

Left: Soviet ships in Havana harbor which aroused the CIA's curiosity. Right: The house in Marianao where "Bob" and the author lived until their cover was blown.

The U.S. Embassy in Mexico City in 1961, where the CIA station was located.

The park in Mexico City where the author met with agents he controlled.

11

CRASHING FIDEL'S HIDEAWAY:
Our Man in Havana Disappears

THE sudden finale to my stay in Cuba was fashioned by another of those odd twists of circumstance that somehow unwind to absurd consequences. Most times the consequences merit no more than a rueful laugh or shrug of the shoulders. But in this case, while I could shrug off the consequences as far as I was concerned, it was not to be so for others who were affected.

There are many jealousies and frictions among the various operating divisions of the Clandestine Services. The reasons for conflict have their roots in the way in which the Clandestine Services was organized and managed. Operational components (divisions) were broken down into areas: i.e., Western Hemisphere, Western Europe, Eastern Europe, Far East, Near East, Africa, Soviet Union, and later another virtually solo division, the People's Republic of China. It was a fact of life that for the two most important areas from the standpoint of U.S. national priorities, the Soviet Union and the People's Republic of China, operational activity on a sustained basis within them was practically nonexistent. Therefore these two divisions, Soviet and "Chicom," were compelled to conduct their operations against their targets from areas within the jurisdiction of other divisions. The host divisions, then, found themselves in the anomalous position of reacting in their own areas to the priorities and requirements of outsiders.

For example, it was only after pressing priority demands occasioned by the presence of Soviets and Communist Chinese

73

in Cuba that the Western Hemisphere division permitted the monolithic facade of their Havana Station to crack a bit. That accounts for the fact that I, of the Soviet division, and Bryan, of the Far East division, were on hand in Havana when the first little twist of fate took hold.

Probably because Bryan and I were drifters compared to the more stable complement of the station, we were approached one day by the Chief of Station with an attractive offer. The chief, on behalf of a friend, invited us to occupy temporarily his friend's luxurious home in the suburbs, equipped with cook, maid, gardener, hi-fi, two-car garage, etc. — all the perquisites of the good life. We got all that for merely paying the current bills to run it.

Bryan and I enjoyed the commodious and lavish surroundings for about a month. It was a happy arrangement, uncomplicated by our individual routines. Characteristically for officers from two different divisions of the Clandestine Services, we seldom discussed each other's work, operations, or problems. Then, as a complete surprise to me, Bryan was replaced by Bob, an equally nice chap, who added to the good life by being a master mixer of martinis.

Our idyllic home life underwent a startling change one day. Without warning to me, Bryan reappeared at our suburban retreat in the company of three technicians from Headquarters, one of whom had worked with me earlier on the Hotel Rosita operation. Aside from the "old home week" atmosphere that prevailed, it was apparent that Bob had an operation going which was about ready for the "kill." I gathered that the technicians were about to plant a listening device in the floor of an apartment (or office) directly above the office of the New China News Agency of the People's Republic of China, located in a multi-story building in downtown Havana.

At the first get-together, it was somehow agreed that the technicians would remain at the house for the duration of their assignment. Supposedly, the arrangement met some criteria of operational convenience, for, as I well knew, operations of this nature required long planning sessions, drills in technical and security practices, and unencumbered communications among all members of the team. Although I was not asked, I would not have objected. There were more than enough rooms in the house to accommodate all, and the technicians were to chip in to compensate the servants for their extra work. Within a day or two, Bryan returned to Headquarters and life in the suburbs resumed its usual routine.

The bombshell hit early on the day I was scheduled to undertake what turned out to be my last job in Cuba, Operation Treasure Hunt, which set me on the trail of the biggest game of all — Fidel Castro.

An embassy associate and friend, Phil, the same naval attaché who figured so prominently in Operation Ox, had learned from one of his sources that it would be possible to gain entry to a motel cabin in which Fidel Castro had recently stayed to recuperate from an illness. This was the hottest lead to come round in a long time, since in fact Castro earlier had been missing from the Havana scene for several weeks, and the usual rumors and speculation had him anywhere from being in Russia to being in the grave. Here lay the opportunity not only to know the truth of his whereabouts during that period, but if we were lucky, even to discover the nature of his illness. Phil asked me to take over the investigation, although he would accompany me because he alone had been entrusted by his source with the credentials for getting by at the motel. Since the motel was several hours' drive from Havana, we planned to start about ten o'clock on the selected day.

The day began inauspiciously. A frantic telephone call from the station related that evidently something had gone wrong with Bob's operation: The technicians had reportedly been taken into custody by Cuban G-2; Bob's whereabouts were unknown.

Before hurrying to the station, I checked Bob's room; his bed had been slept in. I learned from the servants that he had left the house early. I reported these facts to the Chief of Station and told him all I knew about the operation, the technicians, and events up to the moment.

The time sequence surrounding the capture of the

technicians was blurred: The report of the event itself to the
Chief of Station was sketchy — which only heightened the
alarm felt for Bob, who carried credentials as an employee of
the American Embassy. On the off chance that Bob may not
have been with the technicians, I offered to post myself outside the building where they had presumably been nabbed, to
intercept Bob if he should put in an appearance. I also reminded the Chief of Station of my appointment with the naval
attaché. He agreed that I should stay outside the building as
long as possible.

I shall never forget that vigil, which I maintained for over
an hour. My effort to appear composed and inconspicuous
belied my thoughts. How would the technicians hold up if
they were tortured? What information had G-2 extracted from
them? Perhaps at this very moment I was being hunted. An
uneasiness — that at the very least G-2 would have found out
where the technicians had been staying — settled like a cloud
over me. Mechanically following suggested countersurveillance
practices, I ambled leisurely to and fro along my post, peered
into display windows, read my newspaper unseeingly, straining
to catch a glimpse of Bob. But he did not show, and when
someone from the station came to relieve me I left for my
appointment. My uneasiness about the house, the irony that
I might become a victim through a quirk of circumstance,
intruded in my thoughts throughout the day.

As Phil and I drove in search of Castro's motel cabin, we
tried to distract ourselves with the beautiful tropical country-
side and the sleepy picturesque Cuban towns along the way.
We skirted the off-limits coastal town of Mariel, a burgeoning
naval base and delivery terminal for many Soviet ships, and
stopped for lunch in a little town that boasted a restaurant.
Although the town, and the restaurant, were plastered over
with pictures of Fidel and the ever-present *Venceremos*
posters, there were no signs of hostility toward us. We had
the feeling that the Revolution had not penetrated very deeply
into this locality.

After about another hour's drive, Phil, following the directions given by his source, left the highway and drove along a

dirt road until he came in view of the motel, situated at the crest of a green hill that sloped to the shining blue-green waters of a picture-book bay.

One person was in the lobby to greet us, and we were quickly informed that no one else was on the premises that day. We did not inquire, and we were not told, who our greeter was or what status he held at the motel. Our host did not appear particularly nervous about his role, and raised no insinuations about a quid pro quo. He told us that the motel was one that Fidel used as a retreat from time to time. He confirmed that Fidel had been there recently for the longest period he had ever stayed, and that he had remained in his cabin the whole time. He said he would take us to the cabin, and we could see for ourselves that Fidel must have been quite sick because there were all sorts of medicines lying around. As we were conducted through the grounds, we were impressed with the surprising lavishness of the motel, considering how remote it was.

We ranged through the several rooms, eager to note the more intimate aspects of how a man like Fidel Castro lived. The cabin had been cleaned up. The bed was made, its cover turned down at the pillow. All of Fidel's personal articles, however, lay where he had left them, including a motley collection of medicine bottles, jars, and tubes. I asked our guide if Castro kept a supply of medicines at the motel. He shrugged uncertainty and said that the ones lying around were empty but hadn't been thrown out yet. When our host wasn't looking, I lifted some samples and dropped them into my pockets. Both Phil and I were keenly aware that few Americans had ever come this close to the personal side of Fidel Castro.

On our return to Havana, I examined the samples. The containers were not as empty as our guide had thought, but held respectable amounts of ointments, liquids, and pills, sufficient for thorough analysis. A definite scoop! Phil bore down on the accelerator, while I daydreamed about the report I would get off to Headquarters as soon as we reached Havana. It was dusk when we arrived, and I asked Phil to drop me off at the embassy although the offices had already closed for the day.

I was let in by the Marine guard and made my way to the station, to find it ablaze with lights and filled with personnel, who descended on me as if I had returned from the dead. It immediately became clear that a crisis was in progress, involving not only my colleagues but me, too. The worst had been confirmed: The technicians were in the hands of G-2; Bob had also been apprehended but, as an official, had suffered only expulsion from Cuba. The newspapers and the radio were ballyhooing the smashing of a spy ring of the CIA. No mention of me yet, but everyone thought that it was only a matter of time before the last link in the chain coupled to the house where Bob and the technicians had lived would be closed.

Worse, no one knew precisely what the state of affairs at the house was, even though Bob had evidently been permitted to collect his things when he was hustled out of Cuba. The Chief of Station decided that I should leave Cuba as soon as possible, the next day. The trouble was that all my belongings were in the house, including identifying documents and scraps of paper on which I kept cryptic records of my own operations and meetings. The resultant discussion boiled down to a reluctant consensus that the simplest way out of the confusion was for me to return to the house for the night, as though nothing had happened, sort out and destroy any incriminating evidence, and return to the station in the usual manner in the morning, ready for departure.

Before I left the embassy that night, my last in Cuba, I left the medications behind with instructions to forward them to Headquarters as soon as possible and to get a report of the trip from Phil.

The unreal aspect of that last night in Cuba was that everything was serene and normal. The servants had gone to bed. Outside was the steady, undisturbed hum of myriads of insects that constituted the stillness of night in the tropics. Inside, unhurriedly, I went about the business of destroying operational notes and appointment pads and any other accoutrements remotely connected to my profession. I stowed my personal belongings — money, passport and other identification papers, letters, and odds and ends — in a flight-bag. And then I went to bed and uneasy sleep. I half expected to hear the police at any moment.

Next morning I took cautious farewell of the house and the servants, who though they knew something was amiss were not unduly alarmed since I appeared to be acting in the accustomed manner. I couldn't help wondering about their fate, although I expected that the Chief of Station, who was known to the servants as a friend of the owner, would not forsake them. I drove to the station, where final arrangements for my departure had been made: a reservation on the first flight to Miami and an alert to Miami Station to pick me up at the airport. It was early afternoon when I said my good-byes, was driven to José Martí Airport, waved to no one in particular from the door of the aircraft, and left the soil of Cuba.

At Miami I was whisked off to the station for a debriefing in depth. Undeniably I felt a glow of excitement and importance as I narrated the chain of events, even though my part in them was fortuitous and peripheral. My head was still brimming with my foolhardy exposure to possible capture outside the building where the technicians had been working, and with the significant intelligence I had collected about Fidel Castro just the day before. Later, I was returned to the airport, where I boarded a night flight for Washington. At six in the morning, I knocked at the door of my home in Bethesda. At least for my family, their "Man in Havana" had returned, and none too soon.

The next day I reported to Headquarters, bursting to tell my story. I should have known something was up when the normal routine of clearing through reception was altered. Instead of being conducted to my own division, I was, as the clerk in reception informed me, to be immediately brought to the Western Hemisphere division. As I was being ushered into the meeting room, into the presence of the chief and other high officials of the division, I sensed that I was hardly to be accorded a hero's welcome. The faces around the table had anything but friendly curiosity about them.

They started to lecture me mercilessly about the grievous security lapse I had committed. My crime, no matter how embellished in that star chamber, came down to one thing: I had permitted the technicians to remain in the same house with case officers. I tried to turn the questioning and accusations toward the facts of the situation and my part in it, but was frozen out completely. The burden of the entire meeting, as I gathered it, was to pin the blame on me personally for having caused the deplorable circumstances that reflected unfairly on the competency of Western Hemisphere division and gave the Agency an unnecessary headache. By the time I left the meeting room my feelings, oddly enough, were not of anger or resentment but of chagrin for those who had put on such a demeaning display of bureaucratic pettiness.

To the best of my knowledge, the technicians were convicted of spying by a Cuban court and remained in a Cuban jail for over a year. During that period the United States government provided for their families and carried on negotiations for their release. After their release, they were brought back to the Agency, although, as was common talk, they were excluded from active assignment. I heard also that some of Bob's Cuban agents, involved in the same operation, fell into the G-2 net. I don't know, but I rather doubt that U.S. representations for release extended to them. A question lingers as to the extent of responsibility and solicitude borne by the Agency toward those agents who get "burned" or hurt in service.

I was naturally anxious to know about Fidel's medications and the story they told of his illness. But I was prevented from pressing my inquiries then. Not long afterward the American Embassy in Cuba was closed.

The operation that I considered the most tangibly productive of all I had performed in Cuba remained in a limbo of official silence. When my colleagues from Havana Station returned to the United States, I could not ascertain from any whom I questioned whether the medications had been forwarded to Headquarters. I never learned even if a report of Operation Treasure Hunt had been sent. The only treasure, it seems, was one stored in my memory.

12

BACK AT HEADQUARTERS:
Professional Musings and Misgivings

IT would be comforting to say that I was able to draw some definitive conclusions about the spy business and the role of the Clandestine Services from my work in Cuba, but in truth, about the most I acquired was an uncomfortable gut feeling that there were apparent contradictions between the Clandestine Services mission in Cuba and the realities I confronted.

One palpable impression I did carry away from Cuba was that it didn't make much difference to anyone along the chain of command whether a case officer achieved successes or not, as long as he went through the prescribed motions. As far as I was concerned that was fine and dandy, because I was no longer quite so sure that "success" by Clandestine Services standards dovetailed exactly with mine. Besides, Headquarters' benign neglect had no bearing whatsoever on the otherwise considerable benefits of the life of the case officer overseas: The pay was good and the fringe benefits excellent, befitting affluent America; the conditions of work were beyond reproach. The activities of the case officer were intrinsically interesting and even enhanced by the Agency's adversary imperatives, which generated a certain air of excitement.

The most self-effacing case officer cannot avoid swelling in his own estimation to heroic dimensions. Consider the position of importance and power he holds: He dispenses money and largesse in the form of salaries and gifts to his agents; he tipples at the finest bars and dines at the most expensive restaurants; he commands the resources of his government by simply whispering the magic words, "operational necessity," and all in the line of duty and on company time. If that doesn't convey a feeling of being bigger than life, I don't know what does.

Then, best of all, there is the image that attaches to the case officer's profession. In the field, he is not considered a sleazy character or a low-down spy. On the contrary, he is lauded as an activist, a doer of great deeds, an oversexed gladiator (thanks to James Bond), a "cold warrior" in the underground fight against evil from without. To friends back home he engenders an image of the frontline defender, the man on the barricades, who risks dangers every day of his life so that the folks back home may be kept safe and secure. Indeed, the image of our "cold warriors" prevails to some degree in more sophisticated circles than the general public — among government officials, the higher echelons of business, industry, academia, and the professions, and notably within the intelligence community. It was a wrench for me to realize that case officers, with few and fortuitous exceptions, led safe if not sane lives and that others took the risks.

By risks, of course, I mean threat to body, life style, and peace of mind. For overseas case officers in countries friendly to or dependent on the United States, there is an absolute minimum of risk. In those countries where the United States wields political clout, about the worst that can happen to a case officer caught *in flagrante* in an illegal act is that he will be returned to Headquarters for reassignment. In friendly countries, such treatment applies to case officers regardless of their "cover," whether in "official" status as employees of the United States government or in "non-official" status with no ostensible attachment to government. Poison pellets are not for them.

For the relatively few case officers who must operate in unfriendly countries, known in the intelligence trade as "denied areas," there is naturally a higher element of risk. But even here, the niceties of *persona non grata* usually apply for case officers who may be detected in transgression of the law, or for those against whom spurious charges may be trumped up by the host country. Incidents in which intelligence officers undergo detention, imprisonment, or punishment stand out as extraordinary exceptions (the downed CIA officers flying a "drop" mission in the People's Republic of China; Gary Powers in a CIA U-2 plane which crashed in the Soviet Union; the CIA technicians in Cuba; and a passel of temporarily restrained suspected Americans in the East European countries).

My experience in Cuba had taught me that it was the agent who bore the risk. The norm for conducting operations is to do so through agents, usually but not necessarily citizens of the country in which the case officer is operating. An agent is "chosen" by the fall of fortuitous circumstances, or by design, according to the access he has to the particular target, personal or physical, or to the means of reaching that target. It is the agent who is at the heart of the operation, who is the prime mover. It is the agent, not the case officer, who does the skulking around where it counts, who dissembles, who puts his life style on the line, and indeed, in some cases, his life. In case of a "flap," or exposure of the operation to local authorities, nine times out of ten it is the agent who suffers. If there are any heroes in this business, the accolades should go to the agent. Of course, although I had discovered that the hero image of the case officer is pure hogwash, I did little in those early days of reflected glory to dispel it.

Little wonder, then, that I experienced a let-down when I resumed my duties on the Latin American desk of the Soviet division. The worst of it was that I couldn't get Cuba out of my mind. I knew that Western Hemisphere division was preparing an invasion, and I felt I had a positive contribution to make. I even tried to transfer temporarily to the Cuban desk of the division, but to no avail. Doors were closed, my requests were buried in red tape. Recalling the hostile reception on my return, I had to accept the distinct possibility that I was *persona non grata* as far as that division was concerned. Most frustrating of all concerning Cuba was the secrecy barrier Western Hemisphere division had erected within the Agency itself and the pretentiousness with which it was hugging the whole Cuban "show" to itself.

No one is more aware of the stupidities of excess secrecy than an intelligence officer, whose professional instincts may be blunted by bureaucratic obtuseness. An incident from my post-Cuba period on the desk exemplifies the perversities of Western Hemisphere division, while suggesting how a case officer's analytical processes work on a counterintelligence problem as well as the difficulties placed in the way.

In the normal course of my duties on the desk I monitored the activities of Soviets all over Latin America. Mexico was unquestionably the most important target. Mexico hosted the largest contingent of the Russian Intelligence Service in Latin America, quite understandably because both the KGB and the GRU used Mexico as a third-country base for running operations into the United States.

One of the operations in Mexico involved a senior KGB officer, against whom we were running a double agent. The Soviet had been manifesting to the agent an extraordinary interest in Cuba and seemed to be preoccupied in critiquing U.S. plans and preparations for mounting the invasion against Cuba. I was impressed by the KGB officer's encompassing grasp of the Cuban problem: Either he knew a hell of a lot more about what the CIA was up to than I did, or he was a fabricator of the first order. The dilemma cried out for solution.

To a counterintelligence officer, this was important on two related counts: to determine whether the KGB evaluation of an international event was an authentic reflection of the KGB's knowledge; and from that, to determine whether the agent was being controlled by the KGB as a channel to the CIA. Even though it is impossible to reach into the mind of someone else, counterintelligence inquiry ignores that barrier by approaching the problem in reverse — by assessing how the mind of someone else reaches us. It is really quite simple, at least in theory. First, it is necessary to establish the validity and importance, or degree of secrecy, of the information that is being passed; then we may gauge the corresponding status of the passer, the agent; and from that we divine the probable state of mind of the opposition service with respect to the agent.

For example, in the instance of the international turmoil surrounding Cuba, if the information derived from the KGB proved to be accurate, important, and not of public knowledge, it would signify that the agent was both well-regarded and trusted by his KGB handler, and it could be assumed that the KGB officer was unaware of our stake in the agent. In that event, the information could well be of extreme significance to those involved in planning the invasion. If, on the other hand, the information was comparatively low-level, of mixed accuracy or no accuracy, and lacked particulars known to be of a classified nature, it spoke little of the stature of the agent in the eyes of his KGB handler, and even less of whether the RIS was aware of our control of the agent. There is an in-between state, when the passer of information will include a mixture of good information and misleading information, the good sweetening the pie so that the bad will be believed. But to the practiced counterintelligence eye, the good is not good enough to obscure the fact that both intelligence services are "working" the same agent and are aware of each other.

I do not deny that this seems inordinately convoluted, but that is how the counterintelligence mind works. Yet the logic of the process produces one inexorable conclusion: Information which meets the tests of accuracy, value, and secrecy is authentic. It was to those tests I wished to subject the information about Cuba that the KGB officer in Mexico was passing, wittingly or unwittingly, through the agent. Even though I had to assume that these same reports were being forwarded to the Cuban desk, I could not assume that they were necessarily being assimilated in Western Hemisphere division or being subjected to the rigorous counterintelligence scrutiny called for. I did not know how to approach the division for a critique of the information according to the test criteria.

Then one day in early April 1961 I received a report from the double agent in Mexico that brought the matter to a head.

He reported that his Soviet contact had mentioned specific [**two words deleted**] for the invasion, actually two [**three words deleted**] which the invasion forces were to strike. Here was something concrete predicated for the future which could act almost as a litmus test to determine the character and properties of the information. I had to get through to Western Hemisphere division.

Through sheer pigheadedness I stayed on the telephone, wending my way past minor officials in the Cuban task force until I finally reached one of the key men. In two minutes I touched upon the compelling reasons for making my call, and requested an opportunity to pursue the matter further in the task force. He said that was not necessary. I must have been rather desperate, for I then asked only for a confirmation or denial of the [**five words deleted**]. After an avoidance of an answer, I heard a curt "thanks" and the sound of the receiver clicking into place.

The invasion was launched on April 17, 1961. The [**two words deleted**] mentioned by the Soviet officer were [**five words deleted**]. Coincidence? I shall never know. Just as I shall never know whether the earlier information from the KGB officer might have been an accurate reflection of details and tactics under consideration by the Cuban task force planners. The point, however, is that professionalism in dealing with information, which ought to be the life-blood of an intelligence agency, was undermined by an amateurish laxity which was allowed to take precedence. It was like the major error that crept into the planning for the invasion, an error which is widely credited for the fiasco which took place. That was the miscalculation that the Cuban people would rally to the support of the invading group. I don't know what my colleagues in Havana were reporting to Western Hemisphere division, but if it was what I could see and feel of Castro's standing with the Cuban people and their enthusiastic support of him, it should have made abundantly clear that assistance to the invading force by the Cuban people was not something to bank on. Wishful thinking has little place in a professional outfit.

Now that Cuba was shelved, I waited, spending time renewing my informal study of a type of operation that interested me — propaganda. Although propaganda operations (which, by definition, are included within "covert action") did not impinge on me to a great degree while I was performing as a desk officer or serving in the field, I confess I have long been a critical observer of them.

The propaganda and deception practiced by the Clandestine Services as a weapon in the Cold War was very similar to that used by the OSS and the Allies in the "hot war." Its purposes were the same — to deceive, to confuse, to cause suspicion, to split the ranks of common enemies, and to incite disturbances or fan dissension in opposition populaces; and, on the positive side, to extol the virtues of the producing country. The term "black propaganda" describes a product that is attributed to a source other than the producer. The term "deception" describes a falsified product as the outcome of a seemingly true or legitimate producing situation. The least deceptive of the types of propaganda is "straight" propaganda, in which the characteristics of the producers are known and their product is authentic, even if selective.

From the little I was able to gather of the activities of the covert action group of the Soviet division, it appeared that their efforts were more akin to "straight" propaganda, supporting such radio outlets as Radio Free Europe and Radio Liberty, both beamed behind the Iron Curtain. The group conducted research into Soviet dissident movements, economic dislocations, evidences of oppression, internal disturbances, etc., presumably to prepare the themes for and lend convincing objectivity to the broadcasts.

I knew even less of the covert action propaganda output of the other divisions, although I did get wind of some fancy schemes. One that was related to me, and I make no claims for its accuracy, was an attempt in Tanzania to feed the flames of conflict between the Soviet Union and the People's Republic of China. China had a strong representation in Tanzania and was extending its influence through massive financial aid and building of a railroad. Perhaps because China was making of Tanzania a "showcase" of the value of doing business with the Chinese, the Soviets there were overzealous to undercut them. What could be better for American interests than to roil the waters of discord and rivalry between the Soviet Union and China, and in the process alert the Tanzanians to the way they were being exploited for political purposes by these two communist countries.

The propaganda plan was simple. Thousands of leaflets were to be distributed in the population centers of Tanzania (it might have been "over" Tanzania, because, if memory serves, the leaflets were to have been dropped from planes). These leaflets were to have been an "authentic" reprint (though rendered in the languages of Tanzania), with genuine signatures, of a Chinese memorandum about the situation in Tanzania, in which the Soviets were excoriated for their under-handed methods of influencing some sectors of the Tanzanian government. I heard that the Technical Services division of the Clandestine Services had come up with an "exemplar" (a copy of a document) that could have fooled the Chinese themselves. I don't know for a fact how authentic the script or its appear-ance was, although I was given to understand that even the paper for the leaflet was in character with Tanzanian standards and not the slick, durable kind that would have meant "made in America."

Although I knew relatively little about the technical details of the project, I am convinced that the above operation and others like it are foregone exercises in futility. I think the only positive result of the Tanzanian operation was that a lot of underprivileged Tanzanians got themselves an unexpected supply of a scarce bathroom luxury. It is certain that the Soviets would have recognized the spurious origin of the leaflets. It is preposterous to believe that the "man on the jungle trail" would have thought twice about the contents of the leaflet, when his first thought was so much more appeal-ing. And as for Tanzanian officialdom, much more concerned with playing off the Chinese and the Soviets for their own benefits, they would have ignored the whole episode, but if convinced of the fine American hand behind it, would have found cause to resent this intrusion into their domestic affairs.

In propaganda operations the means *are* the end. That is another way of describing "operations for operations' sake," or operations without a careful prior reckoning of the result. For propaganda, for deception, there is no way to predict accurately the effect on an uncontrolled audience. How can an outcome be measured? How does one enter the minds of the proposed targets of the operation? How can the expenditure of resources be justified or reconciled on a balance sheet? I think the honest answer is that there is no way.

The confusion in this area stems, I believe, from the ideological intensity generated by the Cold War and from the sense of mission expounded by "psychological warriors" that we are engaged in a battle for men's minds. The conceived threat was the awesome Soviet propaganda machine, which had been pouring out billions of words and spending billions of rubles to denigrate capitalist values, to distract loyalties, and to win over followers to the cause of world communism. There is, so it would seem, only one way to counter such an onslaught — to fight fire with fire, match dollars to rubles.

In the more shadowy world of intelligence, the deception exploits of the RIS were seen as the epitome of excellence in a specialized branch of psychological warfare. When a "Disinformation Bureau" was identified in the KGB, it became possible to assign responsibility and to trace the trail of the forgeries, the "black propaganda," and a whole bag of tricks to sow confusion and disruption in areas being "softened up" for communist inroads. Or so it was perceived. And so it devolved upon the Clandestine Services to exert a psychological counterforce against the enemy.

In the mounting war for men's minds, apparently no one assessing the Soviet effort asked the question: *Which* men's minds? Why did the Soviets expend billions of rubles to beam shortwave broadcasts from Moscow to practically all countries on the globe? Why did they bother to devote broadcasts in the Quechuan language to small bands of Indians on top of the

Andes? Why did they subsidize all those communist newspapers in the West — in the United States, France, England, or
wherever? Was it to win converts over to communism? Did
they hope to brainwash the American people, or plant seeds of
doubt in the Bible Belt? To change Peruvian Indians into
Marxists? To subvert the countries of the West, ripe for revolution? I think not. The Soviets wouldn't spend one kopeck
for spreading the word about Marxism, or communism, or
for peddling "dangerous thoughts" unless there was something
in it for the Soviet Union itself, some hard tangible benefit
that the Soviets could reasonably expect as a fallout. It *would*
spend those billions of rubles (which it has been doing ever
since 1919) to maintain the allegiance of communist parties
to the Soviet Union, to gain from that allegiance a worldwide
claque to support the policies of the Soviet Union, to furbish
an image of strength and power on a world scale, and to demonstrate to its own people and the peoples of the communist
bloc that, indeed, through its good works of spreading communist ideas to benefit all mankind it deserves its place of
leadership and the preservation of its beloved leaders. The
minds it seeks to win (and hold) are those already in the
communist fold.

A failure to recognize the self-serving, driving force behind
Soviet propaganda can lead the combatants against that propaganda into tilting at the wrong windmills, with the usual
ineffective results, or worse, can sometimes turn out to be
damaging or counterproductive. Certainly, this was so in the
scandal that broke in 1967 over a relatively minor and prosaic
kind of covert action operation by the CIA: the use of "dum-
my" American foundations to fund operational employment
of American individuals and organizations overseas. The purpose of the exposed operations was simply that of matching
decibels with the communist propaganda apparatus. Students
representative of the universities of the United States were recruited through "cut-out" student leaders, rounded up, briefed
on their duties, and dispatched on all-expenses-paid tours to
international conferences to register opposition to communist
factions attending. In a similar gambit, American labor union

representatives were selected to engage communist labor factions at international conferences, assemblies, or other forums. Since it would not do for them to be known as agents of the CIA, a few cover organizations with pure and virtuous-sounding names were set up to dole out the money. Really, as such matters go, pretty innocent stuff.

But the flap that occurred when the story broke aroused wide suspicion that the CIA was behaving like an invisible government that was subverting the American political process and trampling the good name and integrity of the United States in the mud. A high-level committee including the then Director of the CIA was quickly appointed to look into the affair. Its final recommendations enjoined the CIA from future participation in such dubious "domestic" practices and cast a shadow on Agency participation in the funding or sponsoring of legitimate American-based enterprises. From the point of view of the Clandestine Services, it must have seemed like a high price to pay for only trying to give the edge to the United States in the battle for men's minds.

After some time at Headquarters, I decided that it was about time I beefed up my own professionalism. So, on a part-time basis I took additional courses in Spanish at the State Department's Foreign Language School. When I was finished, I enrolled in the Clandestine Services training program which I should have taken earlier as a prerequisite for foreign assignment. It was about mid-September 1961 when I started.

The operational training course lasted about four or five weeks and was given at a secluded site in southern Virginia called "The Farm." It consisted mainly of classroom study of theory and cases pertaining to the major branches of intelligence: espionage, counterintelligence, political action, and propaganda. There were field exercises in mapping, arms familiarization, surveillance, and countersurveillance. It was not particularly taxing, although the instruction was decidedly professional. Then, too, I had the enormous advantage of already having been exposed to operations. The facilities, the food, the entertainment and physical fitness programs were all top-notch.

Tanned and educated I returned to Headquarters in the middle of October. The chief called me into his office not long after my return from training and popped the question innocently enough, considering that it was going to change my entire life: "We need someone to fill in at the Mexico Station for two months while Bert (the Soviet division's case officer) goes on home leave. Can you go, right away?" I was excited, but it meant that I would be away from my family again, so I asked the chief if I might talk the proposition over with my wife. We decided the question in terms of what we thought the temporary assignment might mean for my career, and before I knew it I was packed and off again, this time for the "hottest" station in the Western Hemisphere.

13

OFF TO MEXICO CITY:
Short Tour

THE plane arrived over Mexico City Airport late at night, and as it banked for landing I could see the enormous spread of lights and movement below. That moment reminded me of my first landing at José Martí Airport in Havana, where the city lights had appeared so friendly and beckoning. By comparison, a first glimpse of Mexico City showed lights that seemed more brittle, more metallic, colder. Somehow for me the difference between the two countries was captured in the twinkling and glow of their lights.

I stayed in the Hotel Francis directly across the street from the United States Embassy, which occupied the upper floors of a tall office building. My cover for this assignment was the thinnest, as a temporary employee of the embassy.

Bert, the case officer I was temporarily replacing, remained a few days before departing to break me in and to turn over to me his going operations. Although he probably didn't realize it, he had already figured in my destiny. He had been the case officer who had vacated the Latin American desk at Headquarters and whose position I had taken for my first operations job. Now, it was he, again, who was nudging me on to the next rung of the career ladder. Moreover, we hit it off well together. Before Bert left for the States, he told me of his plan to request another case officer for the station's Soviet affairs, intimating that if his request worked, my temporary tour at the station would give me an edge for the job.

In whirlwind fashion, Bert whisked me around to meeting

places with his agents. One meeting took us up to ten thousand feet, overlooking the valley of Mexico. Another was in a rundown restaurant in an unsavory part of town. Others were at bars around the city. A few were held in hotel lobbies. One was arranged in the office of one of his agents! Before each meeting, Bert profiled the agent for me, pointing out his human qualities, his strengths and failings. I was familiar with most of his cases from my work at Headquarters, but Bert brought them to life, enabling me to get a handle on each more rapidly.

When Bert left, I began to poke around in the nooks and crannies of this smooth-running, well-organized station, and the more I poked the more impressed I became. In Havana I had to spend long hours in a parked car just to glimpse a Soviet. Not so in Mexico City Station; that kind of information came pouring in without my moving a finger. Photographic coverage of [four words deleted] of the Soviet Embassy provided daily reports of the sighting of individual Soviets and others, with accompanying photographs. From certain [two words deleted] lines to the Soviet Embassy, the station had a complete daily account of conversations between Soviets inside the embassy and callers from without. The station regularly received on a sustaining basis passenger lists of arriving and departing planes at Mexico City Airport. Along with the steady stream of reports from a multitude of agents and even strangers on their contacts with Soviets, it is no exaggeration to say that Mexico City Station knew more about the comings and goings and behavior patterns of the Soviets in Mexico than did the Soviet Embassy itself.

The mountain of material exacted a heavy cost to the case officer in the sheer amount of time required to plough through it. In addition, Headquarters inundated the case officer with guidances on specific cases (the kind I used to send to stations) as well as a variety of studies on the Russian Intelligence Service, tradecraft, publications of the Agency on Soviet politics, policy, economics, culture, etc., advance "leads" to Soviets whose paths might cross Mexico, and intelligence requirements. This bulk of routine, non-operational matter that the case officer must digest gives a good picture of the bulk of a spy's activity abroad. At the very least it should clothe James Bond in a gray flannel suit.

The realities surrounding this extraordinary piling up of information about the other fellow (and make no mistake about it, the RIS is similarly engaged) are significant. Such monitoring activity is undertaken with the full knowledge that the Soviets are aware of it; the Soviets know their premises will be photographed, they anticipate that their telephone lines are tapped, they are as clever as we in recognizing dual control of double agents. The station operates under the same guidelines; it assumes that the RIS is photographing the comings and goings of our diplomats, that our telephone lines are tapped, that the Soviets have a good idea of the functioning of a Clandestine Services station and are aware of the identities of CIA personnel. Since these are the prevailing assumptions on both sides, it stands to reason that few secretive moves would be exposed to the camera's eye and that precious little classified information would be confided over a telephone. Why then all the fuss, all that effort, all that expenditure of case officer time?

The answer is a horrendous affront to the professional intelligence community. It lies deep in the furtive psyche of the "dirty tricks" practitioner, who in the closed world of clandestine intelligence enjoys the highest stature and the most acclaim. The dirty tricks specialist is convinced that nice guys finish last in the intelligence business, as in any enterprise in this sinful world. He is equally convinced that the way to achieve intelligence goals is through non-conventional, under-handed, devious, deceptive, and above all secretive tactics — sophisticated ways that are both unknown and unavailable to the nice guy. He believes, and thus becomes the prime victim of deception, that anything collected by the sneaky route has intrinsic worth. A mind so prone to plunge into wiretaps, bugs, surreptitious entries, deceptions, and the like becomes a captive of the clandestine mentality.

Mexico gave proof that it is the agent, not the case officer, who supplies the generating force of an operation. The moral is clear: it is up to the case officer to find the agent or to have the agent find him. The major block to the case officer's voyage of discovery is that he fears to dip his toes into unknown waters; he cannot know the trustworthiness or caliber of individuals in the sea of people who surround the target. Fortunately, it is the agent who usually seeks out the case officer.

Someone walks into the American Embassy and states that he or she has a matter of confidence to discuss. The person is immediately shunted to an officer of the CIA field station located within the embassy. The applicant states that he has become involved in some way with a Soviet or other foreign communist representative, or he has come into possession of incriminating communist materials, or whatever. He is afraid that "the United States" may not approve or understand, and so he wishes to make a clean breast of it. (More likely, he is motivated by the fear that the embassy may uncover derogatory information about him when he next applies for a permit to travel to the United States.) If the informant's contact proves to be a Soviet, then the Soviet division's case officer representative steps in.

More than likely the case officer already knows a great deal about the mentioned Soviet target; that is one of his ongoing jobs — to keep track of Soviets and their activities in his area. If the Soviet is a known or suspected intelligence officer of the RIS, the case officer can smell the possibilities of developing a double agent operation. If the Soviet is not within the circle of known or suspected RIS operatives, the case officer senses a possibility of ferreting out just how close the Soviet is to that circle, especially if the target is a relatively new arrival to the area. Since the assumption is that all Soviets stationed or temporarily abroad are likely compromised or coopted for use by the RIS, case officers tend to regard every operation against Soviet personnel within a counterintelligence framework.

The skilled case officer who rapidly assesses both the applicant and the operational potentialities can then and there make his pitch for cooperation, thus initiating the recruitment.

There may be extended discussion of what is meant by "cooperation" and what, if any, risks are entailed, but in the end the applicant usually accepts the proposition of continuing his contacts with the target under the guidance of the case officer. With the recruitment the operation is under way, subject only to Headquarters security clearance by the CI staff. Preliminary arrangements for subsequent meetings with the agent, under suitable conditions of clandestinity, and the hint of reward generally suffice to put the agent in the proper frame of mind for engaging in secret work.

The objective of typical Soviet CI cases is to identify the personnel, activities, and method of operation of the RIS or its coopted personnel. The underlying purpose is to harass the opposition RIS, to render its operations ineffective, and, it is hoped, to expose RIS officers to the point that they may be declared *persona non grata* by the host country. The assumption behind uncovering RIS operations is that RIS espionage and political action resources anywhere in the "free" world are directed primarily toward the United States.

Enthralled as I was by the volume of information collected at Mexico City Station by secret means, I did not realize at the time what a waste it was. Nor did I have time for such reflection, since keeping Bert's operations going was almost a full-time job in itself.

Mexico City Station's efforts against the Soviets had long emphasized double agent operations, from which it might be learned to what extent the KGB or GRU were pressing their agents to penetrate U.S. circles, or to collect information on sensitive U.S. activities in Mexico or the United States.

Any case officer contemplating a double agent operation is convinced, or should be, that the opposition probably knows that he is an intelligence officer of the CIA. Indeed, there is always the tantalizing possibility that the walk-in agent is a "plant" by the RIS. If so, that only heightens the competition. What ensues may be likened to a chess game, American Intelligence Service versus Russian Intelligence Service, in which moves and countermoves are studied, projected, and applied. That is probably the simplest description of what double agent operations are — games. Far from being sinister encounters, they usually provide under their mantle of high purpose and mission (on both sides) many opportunities for fun and frolic. Not only I, but other case officers I have known, candidly write off double agent operations as "fun and games."

The course of a double agent operation is fairly well charted. It will wax or wane as the case officers on both sides assess the relative costs involved, or, put another way, the relative damage to the other side. Any move by the opposition through "his" agent to tie up the resources of the other side, to instigate costly investigations, to drain money, to pass along "deception" information, etc., is viewed with the suspicion it deserves. The countering case officer will then try to turn the operation in a direction that will have the same effect on the opposing service. The object of the exercise seems to be to maintain the pace of the operation, to keep it from going sour. Under this compulsion, the case officer himself is tied to a steady pace of clandestine meetings and "holding hand" sessions with his agent, as well as to putting an overload of demands on Headquarters for support. Double agent operations, too, seem to cast a spell over project reviewers and inspire Clandestine Services purse-watchers and auditors to relax their normally prudent oversight of the budget.

At times of international stress, flash points of conflict or confrontation, or threatening moves of Soviet policy and power in the world arena, it is the custom to use the double agent operational window on the Soviets to elicit a "Soviet" view of the disturbing events. The theory is that a clever agent (or case officer) will be able to extract inside information from his Soviet contact. Resultant information is dutifully reported to Headquarters. There, the burden of evaluating the responses is left to the proper processing units. Mission accomplished.

Two examples of double agent operations I ran while on this tour are representative of the more sophisticated, more devious type and of the more routine, bread-and-butter type. One agent, whom I shall call "Fusion" because he seemed destined to serve that function, was a mature, polished Latin American who formerly had been [two words deleted]. He was still very much a part of the diplomatic community scene in Mexico City, was welcomed at most diplomatic functions, and was friendly to and often sought out by U.S. officials for his expertise in Latin American affairs. It was undoubtedly Fusion's entrée to American diplomats that attracted the KGB and led to his recruitment by Soviet intelligence. His KGB handler was constantly giving him assignments to find out the American "position" on various important political happenings around the world that involved the U.S.S.R. Naturally, we worked closely with this agent to censor and/or tailor the contents of the reports he would be turning over to his KGB mentor. Such "pass" or "feed" material had to be plausible in terms of what a person of Fusion's political acumen might have been able to worm out of the Americans, and usually had to be linked with specific verifiable encounters with American diplomats that Fusion had had on specific occasions. Our underlying, sustaining purpose was to maintain his credibility and establish his worth in Soviet eyes, against that day when we might wish to deceive and mislead the Soviets on a particularly significant issue.

That day had arrived before Bert left and continued with me in the midst of it. The issue of the day was one that had boiled up recently (October 1961) when Khrushchev in addressing the 22nd Congress of the Communist Party of the Soviet Union seemed to have dampened the crisis over Berlin and to have trumpeted to the world another reprieve on his signing a peace treaty with East Germany. Those mollifying sentiments came at a time when the United States and the rest of the world were still reeling over the spectacle of the Berlin Wall, which had been erected in mid-August. It appeared that Fusion's KGB officer (as would be likely with KGB officers elsewhere) had been instructed to canvass official U.S. reaction to these latest Soviet moves concerning Berlin and East Germany.

Since case officers are not credited with knowledge of the big picture, the play of feed material in such circumstances devolves upon CIA Headquarters in conjunction with the State Department. The procedure goes something like this: The Clandestine Services provides the details of the operation and the agent, including past history of similar gambits; the State Department or the Office of Current Intelligence of the CIA, briefed on the channel to the Soviets, provides the script; the case officer in the field rehearses the agent on the script and stages, if necessary, a plausible scenario in which the agent might have acquired the information. Care must be taken here, because Soviet diplomats are often present at the functions which serve as the contact locale between the agent and American diplomats. Locally, American diplomats are usually clued in to the charade.

The feed operation is designed to provoke a response from the opposition, especially in the form of relevant new requirements put to the agent from the KGB. When the opposition's follow-up requirements are known, they are then subjected to esoteric analysis to determine gaps in the opposition's store of information about an issue or to reveal areas of deep concern and anxiety on the part of the Soviets. Further, the findings are construed as indices of Soviet intentions or preferences in a given situation.

I did my part in carrying along the Fusion operation, but what I saw only confirmed my views of the shortcomings of propaganda operations. The deadly sin of the feeder is not only his obliviousness to a non-measurable impact on the opposition service, but a similar obtuseness in gauging objectively the range of the opposition's impact on him. In simpler language, the same CI mentors at Headquarters who prepare the feed material for use by our agents can be quite gullible when they are on the receiving end of it. I suppose it is part of the "nine feet tall" syndrome, but the counterintelligence mind tends to attach significance to the statements or opinions of any Soviet, more so an officer of the RIS, on the simple thesis that a Soviet individually mirrors the thinking of the Kremlin. I'm afraid that in any exchange of deceptive materials on that basis, we wind up the losers.

An operation I handled at the other end of the double agent spectrum, of the bread-and-butter variety, was much more absorbing than Fusion. There were no lofty intelligence pretenses about the operation, and the personality of the agent, his warmth and good nature, evoked my personal regard. I shall call this agent "the Horse," which was the nickname, not the code name, we actually used.

The Horse was a likeable guy, not insignificant in a fruitful agent/case officer relationship. He was still a minor, if faded, celebrity among [two words deleted] circles, good-looking, earthy, charming, enthusiastic in his role as agent, and, perhaps most important, married [three words deleted]. The Soviets had latched on to him quite by chance, and from the beginning had tried to use him, through [three words deleted], to obtain simple data about the United States Embassy in Mexico. When that didn't pan out too well, the agent's KGB handler tried valiantly to get the Horse to seduce some Mexican employee of the embassy who presumably would then fetch whatever the Horse wanted. At the moment we were fending off every hare-brained scheme of the KGB to use the agent's considerable talents in effecting a penetration of American installations or personnel.

Every meeting with the Horse was a delight. His dramatization of the spy game, accompanied with gestures, was refreshingly naive. Although a happy-go-lucky person, the Horse was having personal problems in maintaining a living and providing for his wife, whom he adored. As trifling as the operation was, I found myself straining to make life easier for him. Although I couldn't raise his salary, I managed to get advances when he needed it. I tried to give whatever sound advice and counsel I could to help him work things out. And then the operation itself took a turn that seemed to provide the perfect answer: convince the KGB to pay the Horse more and more for services rendered. In our meetings, he and I worked out sob stories, expense accounts, risk factors, anything that might pry a buck out of the KGB. The wonder of it was that it worked. The Horse was beginning to get more money from the Soviets than he had before, and he certainly was getting no further in his business for them. What a great game it was!

But it takes two to play a game. What of my opposite number in the KGB? Was he being snookered? I doubt it. I'm convinced that the KGB officer who was running the Horse was just as conscious that the operation wasn't really going anywhere, was just as charmed with the agent as Bert and I, and was just as concerned for the welfare of the agent and his wife as we. This bread-and-butter operation was buttered on both sides.

I look back on that brief but busy first tour in Mexico as a period of concentrated learning about the intelligence business. One thing I learned from the cram course in double agent operations was that the Clandestine Services and the RIS were much alike, both in human resources and methodological approaches — like two teams of sweepers working opposite sides of the same street. Naturally, that was the kind of feeling one kept to one's self.

14

PERMANENT MOVE TO MEXICO:
Non-Official Cover

THE first inkling I had that Bert's petition for a new Soviet affairs officer in Mexico might succeed was when I was taking leave of the Chief of Station at the conclusion of my tour. He commended me for the job I had done and said he would be pleased to recommend me for the case officer slot that was in the mill.

Back home I was immediately plunged into the logistical nightmare involved in the move of Agency headquarters from its weatherbeaten wooden buildings along the Mall in Washington to its gleaming new stone fortress in Langley, Virginia. There was little time or opportunity to think about anything else until I was settled in to the new quarters assigned to the Soviet division. Then one day, about the end of February or beginning of March 1962, I was informed that I had been selected for assignment as a case officer to Mexico, and that I had to work up my cover at once. It had been decided that I was to go under what is called non-official cover; that is, without attachment or ties to any official United States installation. Actually, my cover arrangement was more accurately called deep cover, because ostensibly I would be making a private, personal move to Mexico. I and my family were to transfer to Mexico seemingly for retirement purposes, which under Mexican law could be accommodated by [four words deleted] status. That was all I had to do to work up my cover – apply for [two words deleted]. I was a guinea pig in this experiment since this was the first time this particular gimmick was being used for cover purposes.

I was never fully filled in on why the cover was selected. Normally, cover slots for Clandestine Services personnel abroad are found within the framework of the State Department. It may have been that the State Department resisted placing another CIA spook on its roster. If so, Mexico City Station would have had to examine other possibilities. I might have been given business cover by being put on the rolls of an American firm doing business in Mexico, but that has the disadvantage of putting time and effort into carrying out business duties in order to live up to the cover. That cover, too, is quick to raise suspicions among other employees, who are competitive with a newcomer in their midst who may be underqualified to do the job.

The [one word deleted] idea undoubtedly appealed to the station, because it opened up a whole new vista for beefing up the complement of the station and providing replacements. It was geared to the older and more mature case officer whose age bracket might plausibly permit him the luxury of retiring to Mexico with an annual income of ten thousand dollars. Under Mexican law the [two words deleted] could earn no money in Mexico for a period of five years. From the station's point of view that was great; the case officer was free as a bird and could devote all the time necessary to his clandestine work. The only precaution necessary, not for the Mexican authorities but for the circle of friends and acquaintances that the "retiree" might encounter in the American community and elsewhere, was a plausible explanation for how the retiree was occupied in the Mexican scene. In my case it was decided that I would palm myself off as a writer. As a matter of fact, in my five years in Mexico I wrote numerous short stories and several novels, and could explain that I was doing research along certain lines to account for some of the bizarre situations in which I found myself, and others found me.

I began by finding out from the Mexican Embassy in Washington what was required. The whole family would have to get United States passports; that would be easy. The Mexican government needed copies of original birth certificates, marriage certificate, and official witnesses to the fitness of my character, satisfied by certification by the police. The major qualification for [one word deleted] status in Mexico was proof that I had a sustaining income (not wages or salary) of at least ten thousand dollars. The cover division of the Clandestine Services worked out a sweet deal for me. They got a major [one word deleted] to certify that I derived over ten thousand dollars per year from various (spurious) income-producing sources, which the [one word deleted] itself handled for me. It was a sweet deal because it made life much easier for me in Mexico City; the [one word deleted] would receive my regular paycheck and transfer the amount to [three words deleted] in Mexico City, and all I had to do was to carry the account in the [one word deleted] bank and pick up whatever money I needed. Also, to satisfy the Mexico government every year regarding the income I had received, I had merely to show what had been deposited to my account in Mexico.

Absorbed as I was in preparing my cover and feeling grateful for the Agency's professional assist, I was hardly prepared for a development that might have dashed the whole plan into the garbage heap. The villain was the Western Hemisphere division, which suddenly seemed unwilling to endorse my move to Mexico on security grounds. The case the division had prepared against me stipulated that I and my family had grossly violated security by loudly and frequently broadcasting from the porch of my home the particulars of my Mexican assignment. I protested to my accusers that it simply was not true, and demanded to know the specific basis for the charges. Security is an unfunny kind of thing; a charge alone is a damnation, and the burden of proof is on the accused to remove the blemish. Fortunately, my own division, the Soviet division, backed me up and lent weight to my demands for verification of the charges. The result was a retraction by the Western Hemisphere division; they had got their "facts" wrong; it was some other CIA employee (not of the Clandestine Services) in my neighborhood who had been loudly indiscreet in a matter totally unrelated to Mexico. The case was closed, but I cannot escape the feeling that it was trumped up by the Western Hemisphere division in its lingering resentment over the part it alleged I had played in the capture of the Agency technicians in Cuba.

I did not know when I applied to the Mexican Embassy on this seemingly clear-cut matter that I was embarked on a never-ending bureaucratic river of frustration. Unmentioned fees would crop up all along the processing of our papers and call for heroic efforts after payment to get the processing moving again. By contrast, the Agency's cover division and finance office went all out to smooth the process and sweeten the pie. As an officer under non-official cover, I received a differential in pay. Every official fee and even non-official expense like a bribe (the Mexicans call it *mordida*, a bite) was paid for unhesitatingly. And I received all the perquisites of residence abroad, major living expenses, schooling for the kids, language improvement courses, utility installation fees, and the like.

Never fully explained until we arrived at the border was the small matter of taking our car into Mexico and the awesome requirement that that same car would have to leave Mexico no matter what. (This we little appreciated until we had driven on Mexican gasoline, in Mexican traffic, on Mexican roads sometimes in the clouds, in a three-carburetor job that a Mexican could not repair with a hairpin.)

It was mid-June 1962 when we were permitted to enter Mexico, but only after the payment of unanticipated high personal fees that required wiring our bank in Mexico City to send pesos. The finalization of our papers took many weeks. Months after arriving in Mexico City, all of us had to return to San Antonio, Texas, to retrieve our final papers. The red tape involved in getting out of Mexico for the San Antonio trip and then getting back in was unbelievable. I was able to vent some of my frustrations in the report I compiled for the station to serve as guidance to other case officers taking the same route.

Upon reflection, I wonder why the Mexican government, which was seemingly so anxious for the Yankee dollar, put so many obstacles in the way. At any rate, after the first border crossing in June, all temporary frustrations were temporarily circumvented. Our three-carburetor Pontiac, all carburetors choked with dirty gasoline, barely staggered into Mexico City. I was ready to go to work.

15

A KOOKY BUSINESS:
Agent in Shock

IN every sense, organizationally and administratively, Bert, the inside man, was my boss even though the position he was put in of servicing my every need on the outside might make it seem that I was calling the shots. But it was Bert who initiated the operations and assigned and guided my part in them. It was Bert's responsibility to pass on to me all support information and technical equipment that were necessary to discharge my obligations. He was the pipeline for keeping me abreast of Agency regulations that affected me as an employee. And he even cut me in on stateside items like American tobacco that were available to State Department personnel at reasonable prices. It was fortunate for me that Bert was understanding and unpretentious, with a delicious cynical humor about the absurd business we were in.

The Agent in Shock
Even though I had been on the counterintelligence scene in Mexico for some time, I was glad that it was someone like Bert with a sense of humor who broke the news to me of a high-priority, hush-hush experimental operation that Headquarters had decided to try out in Mexico. I had heard of many kooky things in my day, but this one took the cake. The operation was a brainchild of the counterintelligence staff, who thought it was just about the greatest boon to its work ever to have come along the pike.

The CI staff had exclusive control over the process of clearing agents for use (what the British call "vetting"). The staff conducted inquiries about prospective agents and double agents (the latter because of its congenital paranoia about possible penetrations by the opposition). It consulted files and dossiers; it studied each case individually, and only then would rule whether an agent could be used, and to what limits.

The CI staff had in tow a young psychiatrist who claimed that he could produce a hypnotic state in an instant of shock to the subject. He had evidently convinced the staff of its feasibility. Such a feat opened up wide vistas of utilization by the staff, particularly in the area of its prime concern — the bona fides of Clandestine Services agents. Under hypnosis, the agent was compelled to reveal the truth, thus putting to rest the doubts that always remained after studying the scattered and elusive evidence contained in a dossier or a file. Best of all, the method of putting the subject under instantaneous hypnosis was practical and adaptable to the agent situation, with the significant added factor that the agent would remember nothing of the experience. The time had come for a field test with an agent.

The reason that Mexico was chosen for the experiment was that the station had a prime candidate, a double agent whose honesty was in question, and had a psychiatrist who spoke Spanish. The selectee was an agent of mine whom I shall call Ignacio. He was a young man, a bachelor, and a native of [one word deleted]. On his first contact with Mexico City Station he offered to become a double agent against the KGB, which had recruited him and was paying him handsomely. We accepted and informed him of our method of payment: He was to turn over to us the dollars received from the Soviets, which we would exchange for other dollars (we were interested in the serial numbers). While I was directing him, he moaned and groaned about the method of payment, and continually pressured for additional money for his labors and the high risk he was running with the Soviets. Part of our problem with Ignacio was that he spoke no English and had little patience with my fumbling efforts to nail down meaning in the Spanish language.

The reports Ignacio showed us before he turned them over to the KGB in Mexico were so low grade and trivial we could not figure out why the Soviets paid him so much — but we dared not let him go until our curiosity had been satisfied.

The counterintelligence staff representative who had come to Mexico City to pave the way for the test operation laid down the scheduling of it, depending on when I could produce Ignacio in Mexico City. With little more than Ignacio's home address, I set off for [one word deleted] to search him out and induce him to come to Mexico City without raising any suspicions on his part.

On my arrival I registered at one of the better hotels, complete with indoor pool and sauna. That evening I made a telephone call to the number I was given for Ignacio's address. The person who replied said that Ignacio was not at home and seemed on the verge of concluding the conversation. I rushed on to say that Ignacio would want to see me very much, I gave the name I used with him, and said I had to see him immediately. The woman at the other end of the line seemed to be impressed, but she said that Ignacio was away, and she didn't know when he was going to return. I asked, and was granted permission, to come by the house the next day.

The woman who let me in to the rather shabby little house seemed to be in her mid-forties. (I don't know what her relationship was to Ignacio.) I repeated the urgency of seeing Ignacio, and said I would pay for any means she could use to reach him and tell him I was here. I gave her some money, and told her to work it out, but to get to Ignacio without fail. I left her the name of my hotel.

It was a weekend, and I had carried the effort to locate Ignacio as far as I could at the time. I hung around the hotel all day Saturday, hearing no word. On Sunday I decided I needed air, and so took a trip to a nearby ancient city of picturesque ruins. The next day I received a call from the woman: Ignacio had been contacted and would be back probably the next day. Great; progress was being made. I called [two words deleted] Station and had a meeting with one of the case officers. The station had been advised by

Mexico City Station to extend any help I needed, but was told little beyond the fact that I was engaged on a highly important, sensitive mission. The case officer was duly impressed when I divulged some of the details to him. In the evening, I popped in to what looked like a rundown opera house just at showtime and saw an excellent performance of Swan Lake.

Ignacio called me the following morning. He was agitated, confused, and apprehensive, but wouldn't tell me why over the phone. We set a meeting for lunch. Before I could begin to hand him a story of why I had come, he thrust a telegram at me. As I started to read it (in Spanish), he said the Russians wanted him to come to Mexico at the end of the week. The telegram identified the sender with a Russian first name. Was that why I had come? I said, "Of course not. I am here for a much more important reason," and I beamed at him as I told him that my bosses were so impressed with him that they wanted to meet him in person. I laid it on thick (straining my Spanish to the limit) to inform him that they wanted to do him honor. I said it was just perfect that his Russian friend had also called him to Mexico City; Ignacio could kill two birds with one stone (that was tough in Spanish), but to show our appreciation we would provide him with the roundtrip air fare, even though the Russians would also pay him for it. All of Ignacio's confusion dissolved as I counted out one way's worth in dollars. I then set the time and day when I would meet him to take him to see my bosses.

After my meeting with Ignacio, I contacted [two words deleted] Station and got off a cable to Mexico outlining the high points of my mission and advising when Ignacio would be in Mexico. Mexico would act on the information to call in the psychiatrist on time. Very satisfied with the results, I remained over an extra day to check once more with Ignacio that my instructions to him were clear.

Back in Mexico, Bert and I were setting the stage for the arrival of Ignacio. We reserved two adjoining rooms in a motel on the outskirts of the city. In one of the rooms, a colleague and I would be entertaining Ignacio pending the supposed arrival of the big bosses. In the other room, Bert, another colleague, and the Deputy Chief of Station would be waiting with the psychiatrist, ready to send him into his act at the precise moment. The props and the timing were projected in precise detail, down to the position Ignacio would be in, his distance from the door, the exact second of maximum shock. The psychiatrist was thoroughly briefed and rehearsed in every sequence of the operation, including the questions he was to pose to Ignacio while he was under hypnosis. It promised to be quite an evening.

When the evening arrived, I met Ignacio in town and drove him out to the motel. Everything and everybody were already in place. I ushered Ignacio into "his" room, noting that as planned the door had been left unlocked. My colleague, who was standing beside a small round table in the cleared area near the door, was introduced, and he motioned Ignacio to sit in the one chair beside the table. On the table were a bottle of whiskey and three glasses. As we talked, we downed our drinks and took refills, my colleague and I standing and hovering around the table while Ignacio sat. The moment of action was at hand. Simultaneously, my colleague on one side and I on the other side of the chair thrust a foot behind the back legs of the chair and tipped it and its occupant over backwards. In the same instant I flung the door wide open.

Ignacio was squirming on the floor, in some degree of shock I am sure. But it was nothing to the shock that swept over my colleague and me. The door gaped open. No hurtling form filled it; not a sound came through. Realizing that the moment of truth had passed, my colleague and I quickly fought off our perplexity and as if with a single thought bent to pick Ignacio from the floor. I don't remember what we said to soothe his injured feelings (he had not been physically hurt). I think we reinforced each other in conveying to Ignacio that we had become alarmed by some outside noise at the window and had reacted to protect him. While we were thus engaged, the telephone rang. Just a terse word to call it off for the night, but to be sure to keep Ignacio in Mexico City for a few more days. I turned to Ignacio and said that the boss couldn't make it tonight, but wanted very much to see him in a few days. I gave Ignacio some money (more than I would ordinarily have been inclined to), made arrangements for contact in Mexico City, and drove Ignacio back to the city.

Next morning I met Bert; I was bursting to know what had happened. Bert dragged it out. The four of them had gone to their room at the motel and were in high spirits. To pass the time they passed the liquor around, which caused their discussion of the evening's entertainment to become more animated. The three case officers plied the psychiatrist with questions about his art, and he fell to boasting of his technique, its sure-fire success if his accomplices did their part, and how he was going to revolutionize the counterintelligence business. As soon as I arrived with Ignacio, they quieted down and the psychiatrist took his place at the door. They waited; there was no signal (I believe it was a tap on the adjoining wall) of anything that might be amiss; all eyes were on their watches. At the exact second the case officers told their man, "Go!" — and he froze. Bert said he didn't know what the others were doing, but he kept telling the psychiatrist to "go." The psychiatrist stood frozen in his tracks. The case officers peered at the bizarre still-life for an awful moment or two, and suddenly realized that the jig was up. It dawned on them that my colleague and I must be having a hell of a time with Ignacio in the next room, and after somehow having wrung from the dejected psychiatrist his willingness to try again, one of the case officers put in the call to me to fold up for the night.

I was ill with stomach distress, so I didn't participate in the second attempt a few nights later. But I heard about it. This time Ignacio was taken to more grandiose surroundings, which befitted a locale in which he was to meet the big chiefs. A scenario somewhat similar to the earlier one was played out, but with this difference: shortly before Ignacio was due to hit the floor, the psychiatrist chickened out again and refused to go through with the experiment. I regret that I was not around for the postmortems with the psychiatrist.

Operation Surprise

Shortly after I appeared in Mexico City, an operation that had been on the back burner was set in motion. Bert told me about it as we were making our way to a classy restaurant in the tourist zone to recruit our agent. The target of the operation was an intelligence officer of the KGB who occupied an apartment alone in [five words deleted] of Mexico City, fairly close to [three words deleted]. The objective was to bug the Soviet's apartment with the expectation of monitoring the nefarious activities of an active officer of the KGB. The agent we hoped to recruit was an occupant of the same section of the apartment building in which the Soviet lived. Bert told me that after we had recruited the agent (he was that sure of it), it would be my job to run him and fulfill the objective. That didn't sound too onerous; I had had experience in placing bugs.

It was both a pleasure and instructive to watch Bert in action on his own stamping grounds in the recruiting phase of an operation, which according to the book is the most difficult, delicate, and vital part of the process. The agent, whom I shall call Jorge, had already been somewhat groomed for his prospective role; he had been spotted and approached by an old trusted agent of Bert's who vouched for his suitability. We introduced ourselves under phony names to Jorge, who was waiting for us in the restaurant and seemed ill at ease in the unaccustomed surroundings. Bert eased the situation at once, ordering a round of the most expensive drinks in the house. In low key, Bert, who already knew a great deal about Jorge from his agent's report, brought out that we represented the United States government, which was interested in doing something that would be of great benefit to the Mexican government. Jorge, as was anticipated, was quick to mention how much he admired the United States, but that he would do nothing that in any way could hurt Mexico. He added that he was working in his office job to save enough money to go to the United States to settle there [two words deleted]. The rest was easy. What did Jorge think about communism and the communists in Mexico? He hated them; not only were they causing trouble in Mexico, but they were anti-God. Bert went on to mention the Soviet who lived in Jorge's apartment building; had Jorge noticed him? Jorge said he knew there was a foreigner, someone who acted strangely, but not much more. Then, Bert dramatically informed Jorge that the Soviet was an important member of Soviet intelligence, a spy. The conversation then proceeded in lowered tones. Would Jorge join us in working against this Soviet? Yes; but what could he do? Bert's friend here, Mr. Barton (that's me), would tell Jorge what had to be done. And further, Mr. Barton would pay Jorge for his services, so many pesos per month. The figure was enough to give visions of the American dream coming true to Jorge. He agreed to become an agent. The recruitment was over, even before the meal was finished. All that remained was to set up another meeting between Jorge and me to get the show on the road.

That operation lasted over a year. I met Jorge about once a week and paid him his salary like clockwork once a month. The classic approach with a new agent is to ease him into the spying racket with simple tasks like familiarizing himself with the target area (in this case, the location of the target's apartment, access routes to ground or roof, the physical layout of the apartment, history of needed repairs, locking devices on doors and windows, etc.) and establishing a pattern of movement for the target. Every week I would receive a written report covering these items. Since Jorge was at work most of the day, he enlisted the services of his wife, who was at home, with our permission. As it turned out, Jorge's wife really entered into the spirit of the game and became the dominant element in the Jorge team. She learned where to station herself during the day to watch the comings and goings of the KGB officer, and prepared model reports. She nosed around with the superintendent of the apartment building and learned about locks, the layout of the target's apartment, and much more in the way of detail than we had ever asked. She was evidently ambitious and was out to prove it.

Months after the operation had started, when it became difficult for Jorge to make meetings because of a busy season in his office, his wife came instead. She was a young woman, strikingly pretty, darker complexioned than most Mexicans [five words deleted], who, when she appeared at meetings in high heels, in her finery, and lavishly but artfully made up, was likely to attract attention. That posed a problem for me, in case I were to be seen with her in my usual haunts where friends or acquaintances were normally to be found also. Therefore, I went Mexican, meeting her in darkened bars to be found in typically Mexican hotels. After we discussed her reports, and I coached her on gaps that had to be filled, she turned to talking about herself, her life with Jorge, her feeling of being unfulfilled (she was extremely sensitive about her dark complexion). After the first few meetings, probably from the air of intrigue that surrounded us, the darkened bar, the drinks, the opulence and power seemingly inherent in the *Americano* (me), and perhaps most important, her questing ambition, she made it apparent that she was turning toward me as her salvation. I eased her out of that notion as gently as possible, called Jorge at his place of work and scheduled spot meetings with him, and gradually got the operation back on track. I never mentioned the episodes to Jorge, and I never knew from him whether there had been any repercussions at home from his wife's behavior. Shortly before the operation terminated I saw the two of them together, and there was no inkling that anything was amiss. That had been a wrinkle to operational life that I hadn't counted on and that was nowhere to be found in the doctrine on "methods of operation."

A few months after resuming meetings with Jorge, we felt we were ready for phase two of the operation, the final planning for entry to the apartment and placement of the bug. We knew everything there was to know about the Soviet's apartment, the kind of furniture he had, where it was placed, the time his lights went out at bedtime, even the kind of food he stocked in his refrigerator. We had calculated from the pattern of his movements an optimum period during the day when he was likely to be away from his apartment for the longest period of time; we had figured by knowing exact distances of accesses to the apartment a rough time frame for effecting entry; and we knew how long it would take for the technicians to install the bug. Since the Soviet's apartment was [**four words deleted**] below the roof, there was a relatively secure traverse from Jorge's apartment to the roof and across it to the stairway that gave access to the apartment. And we had the perfect monitor, his wife. We took our time planning everything down to the minutest detail, especially security precautions for tailing the Soviet on the day of the operation, laying on diversionary tactics if he should show up unexpectedly at the apartment building, a system of communications from Jorge's base apartment, and contingency plans for repeat attempts if the first should not jell. All systems were "Go."

It pains me to record that for our friend the Soviet all systems were evidently "Go" also. (It was the common jargon between case officer and agent to refer to the opposition target as "friend.") Our friend suddenly moved from his apartment; he was gone, back to the Soviet Union, his tour finished. That finished our operation, too. His apartment was not reoccupied by a colleague, as is often done for replacements or to accommodate other Soviets. Was it fate that did us in, or is it possible that with a little forethought we might have paced that operation differently, or perhaps not launched it at all in the expectation that there was precious little pay-off time for the installed bug in the remaining normal tour period for our Soviet friend?

16

DOUBLE AGENT OPERATIONS:
Gamesmanship With the KGB and the GRU

BOTH the double agent cases I dealt with during my previous temporary tour in Mexico, Fusion and the Horse, I picked up again during my extended assignment. In the case of Fusion, I later turned him over to a colleague in Mexico City Station when it was learned that he would be returning for good to his native country. During the time I had him in Mexico, he was used sporadically in his favorite role of passing on feed material to the KGB, but nothing as elaborate as the earlier probe to establish Soviet intentions concerning Berlin and East Germany. With the Horse I galloped along gaily, letting the reins fall only when I left Mexico.

Double agent cases, I found, often prove that there seems to be a qualitative difference between the civilian KGB and military GRU in operational emphasis. The security-minded KGB is preoccupied with counterintelligence offense and defense against other intelligence services, and with the security of Soviet operations (there have been jurisdictional battles over KGB security oversight of GRU operations). The KGB seems more inclined toward political action operations to influence politics rather than toward mere collection of political information. The GRU, on the other hand, seems bent on the collection of military, scientific, and technological information, and selects its agents and levies its requirements accordingly. The GRU apparently strives independently to maintain a high order of security for its operations, and to hone its own operational techniques and support mechanisms in accordance with its particular mission.

Big Business

One of the most complex, and probably the longest sustained, of the cases run by the KGB and doubled by us in Mexico involved a highly intelligent, personable, energetic, and successful businessman. The KGB must have known that Itzak (the name I shall use for the agent) was very chummy with American intelligence. I had the impression that the seasoned KGB officers who handled Itzak found him a most engaging person, even though they may have sensed that he hated their guts. Itzak took no money from either side, even when in the course of his extensive foreign travel he discharged intelligence missions.

The KGB insistently attempted to use Itzak, or the influence and means at his command, to obtain forms of Mexican identity documents, official credentials for work or business, and background requirements for engaging in various occupations in Mexico, all presumably for the purpose of documenting and providing cover for Soviet agents, who then might use their new identities to gain entry to the United States. Itzak, of course, strung out those requests interminably under our instructions, while at the same time trying to probe from the KGB their intended use of the material. It was a cat-and-mouse game, undoubtedly prolonged and enjoyed by all parties, without any pronounced benefit to either side. Itzak seemed to have the most fun out of it.

Then the operation seemed to have taken a more serious turn. The KGB proposed that Itzak establish a [two words deleted] of his business in [three words deleted], and they were willing to underwrite the entire venture. They were talking about big money now and hinting at the possibility of inserting a few of their own "people" in the business for cover. Itzak, who was a shrewd businessman, had genuine misgivings that the [two words deleted] would be a financial flop and that the Soviets, despite their assurances, would leave him holding the bag. But we urged Itzak to play along, hoping to smoke out the seriousness and extent of the KGB's intentions.

The scenario continued for over two years, from shortly before Bert left Mexico until shortly before I departed, at which time Bert's replacement, Will, figured that American intelligence had been played for suckers long enough by Itzak and the KGB. Will's assessment, I believe, missed the mark widely. There were no suckers in the Itzak operation; not the CIA, not the KGB, and not Itzak. They were simply playing the double agent game to the hilt, the dynamics of which gave great scope to the talents of the protagonists, which was why the intelligence officers of both sides were being paid.

A Flighty Business

The GRU seemed to be absolutely ravenous for information about aviation. The Soviets never tired of two agents whom we doubled (I call them Orville and Wilbur, for obvious reasons), although over the years they received precious little in the way of information that had not passed our strict scrutiny. Orville was a young Mexican businessman, who [four words deleted], and occasionally flew to the United States. Wilbur was an older Mexican who owned an [two words deleted] business, and also traveled to the United States on business.

It's probable that the GRU was interested in Orville because he [four words deleted] and was a flying enthusiast. We suspected that the GRU might be trying to set Orville up as a courier to the United States, but they never took the bait we dangled in front of them. About the best we accomplished was that Orville once or twice was persuaded by his GRU handlers to bring back from the United States some hard-to-get appliances and other items for them. But the GRU intelligence officers loved to talk about aviation with Orville, and because he had this rapport with them we tended to move the operation toward Orville's reporting to us personality profiles of the Soviets he met. Neither we nor the Soviets paid Orville a salary; we paid Orville's operational expenses and never forgot his yearly bonus and gift.

The GRU, understandably, used Wilbur to procure the most up-to-date [five words deleted] available on flight routes and airports in the United States and other areas. What was not so understandable was that the GRU was highly overpaying for them. For the years that Wilbur had been working for the GRU he had evidently supplied them with the complete [one word deleted], and in the year or so I was case officer for Wilbur he was merely filling in the [one word deleted] with the latest releases. It seemed to me that the Soviets could easily have obtained these same [two words deleted] in the United States, at half the cost. But we didn't complain, and when Wilbur was paid in dollars we noted the serial numbers. Wilbur, like Orville, consented to become a double agent in order to cover his dealings with the Soviets and to stand well with Americans.

In a departure from the even tenor of the operation, the GRU once sponsored a trip by Wilbur to the United States to a rather out-of-the-way city where some new revolutionary [two words deleted] was under construction. We coached Wilbur beforehand on the scenario he was to follow when he reached the city, the kind of effort consistent with his credentials that he was to make. Satisfied that Wilbur had gone through the motions we had prescribed, we then allowed him to report to the GRU on his inability to learn about the [one word deleted]. In the double agent game, this counted as a plus for the Americans.

When I left Mexico both these GRU operations were perking along steadily, although Will, who was then the station's inside man for Soviet operations, was considering giving the heave to Wilbur. Will operated according to the book, which cautioned that the RIS was advantaged in double agent operations and that a certain graduating class of the GRU's Military Academy had the sole mission to tie the CIA's Clandestine Services up in double knots.

Illegal Business

I can't recall whether this final double agent operation was run by the KGB or GRU; it had ingredients that might have belonged properly to one or the other. Mexico, we learned from the Abel case, was an established refuge and transit point for Soviet illegal agents of the KGB; it must have served the same purpose for GRU illegals. The Abel case also demonstrated that a KGB illegal net might be served by [one word deleted] personnel as couriers, and that the net could include military people with access to military information. The agent at hand, who in an early stage of the operation seemed to be under grooming as a courier to an illegal net in the United States, later was pushed into becoming an illegal agent himself.

The agent, whom I shall call Hector, was an [two words deleted] who spoke English and Spanish as though they were his native tongues. He worked for a [one word deleted] whose routes included [three words deleted] and the United States. At the time I took over Hector he was being paid steadily by the Soviets and by us, a double take for Hector that we permitted because the operation was shaping up as an "illegal" type and also because we didn't have the heart to cut Hector, who was always crying poverty, not unexpectedly, considering the way he lived it up.

We (and the Soviets) were slaves to Hector's schedule. Half our meetings with him were spent patching together advance notice of the runs that would bring him to Mexico City. That was where we could expect to get some enlightenment about Soviet designs for Hector, after he had had his meeting with his RIS handler. But a new focus crept into the operation, his scheduled trips to the United States, when the RIS began to give him some fanciful assignments. Hector was being trained by the RIS to service "drops," the intelligence term for places of concealment used by generations of spies to deliver messages, materials, money, or anything else that keeps the espionage game solvent. The RIS started Hector off in the most rudimentary fashion: The drops were located close to the [one word deleted] (in the United States) where Hector had a [one word deleted] and contained only colored rocks. Even though the location of the drop might change, on each assignment Hector was requested to bring back to Mexico City a rock of a specified color. This international trade in rocks went on for months. When were the Soviets going to get down to serious business? We were all set to crack down on the toughest prey of all, the illegal. At the proper time, the FBI would swoop down on whoever was servicing those drops (excluding Hector, of course) and we might roll up an entire illegal net.

Our expectations and the rock barrage were suddenly cut short by an even more intriguing move by the RIS, a proposition to Hector to install him as an illegal agent in a foreign country where Spanish was the spoken language. Hector agonized over acceptance; he was loathe to leave his happy-go-lucky existence, or to be separated too long from his wife. He was tempted by the generous salary the Soviets were willing to pay, but he was afraid to break loose from all his ties. We wanted Hector to go through with it; here was our chance to learn the very basics of how the RIS went about putting an illegal agent into the field. That meant RIS methodology in preparing and training the agent, dispatching him, arranging for his cover, setting up his communications, his funding, his possible attachment to a net. We sought to reassure Hector, promising him every assistance to see to it that the Soviets got their agent, even helping him arrange for a cover job in the country he would be sent to. We offered a tempting salary increase, and reminded him that he would also be earning the money he received from his cover job. That did it; Hector would play the game.

The RIS started to prepare Hector for the assignment, and, as we expected, Hector was called upon to locate a job for himself in the foreign country, an important element in meeting the requirements for immigration. Hector reviewed with his Soviet case officer his thoughts about getting a job, the occupations he was suited for, the contacts he had in mind (including a firm that we had already selected and arranged for). Hector went about methodically soliciting a job by correspondence, including all the contacts he had mentioned to the Soviet. It was a protracted process, with Hector giving his RIS case officer progress reports and showing him the ongoing correspondence. At long last Hector had the offer of a job (sure enough, from "our" firm). During that time Hector had precious little training for his assignment, and only when he was ready to leave did the RIS lay on a means of communicating with him by mail. They gave him a large sum of money to sustain him for a long period and promised to resume paying his salary later.

We had arranged for the CIA station in the country to which Hector had been sent to use a case officer to meet with him to transmit our directions and to report the progress of his activities. Hector fit in with his new job satisfactorily enough: although he wasn't deliriously happy about the kind of work, the pay was good. So good, in fact, that after about a month, Hector imported his wife. The Soviets left him to his own devices for several months, although he was sending them periodic progress reports (subject to our best counsel). Just once in the space of almost a year did the Soviets give Hector an assignment, to look over an [three words deleted] in the area, which he duly reported. At the end of the year, Hector returned to Mexico City on furlough, obligingly granted by the Soviets.

When we saw Hector in Mexico City he was depressed. We debriefed him thoroughly on all his experiences, and at the end we were almost as depressed as he. This was at a time when I was ending up my own tour in Mexico. Hector decided to go back, however reluctantly, for another whirl at being an illegal agent for the Soviets, but I had the impression that he wouldn't last, and I wouldn't have blamed him in the least.

I ultimately concluded that the largesse, persistence, and patience with double agent operations exhibited by both contending intelligence services, with little intelligence benefit to either, may signify that they engage in the game for sheer psychological uplift.

17

TYPES OF AGENTS:
Routine at the Mexico City Station

I have likened the conduct of foreign intelligence activities between the United States and the Soviet Union to that of a chess game. The picture is that of two wily opponents, hunched over a chess board, planning intricate moves and probing the defenses of the other. The trouble with that image is that it minimizes or completely overlooks the pieces on the board, the agents, whom I have called the "prime movers" of operations. Agents come in many types.

The Indispensable Agent

There is a kind of agent, rare though he may be, whom every case officer dreams about. He has all the virtues of a Boy Scout, a flair for intelligence work, the values one looks for in a friend, the assurance that comes from a relatively comfortable station in life, and, of course, he is a national of the country in which the case officer is operating. Bert had discovered such an agent, whom I shall call Eduardo, who acted as a partner in many operations, and I had the good fortune to share him.

There were times when operational assists were vital, and only Eduardo could fulfill them. He had attributes that no case officer could ever hope to match: He knew the country; he knew the people; he knew their ways; he knew what influenced them and what repelled them; he knew Mexico and its politics as only a Mexican could know; and he could work fast. I shall recount one operation that we worked on together.

From a minor agent who worked in [seven words deleted] we learned a vital bit of information. The Soviet code clerk, a single man, often came to [two words deleted] in search of a few hours' pleasure with a prostitute. Someone was always able to make the necessary arrangements quickly. Speed was essential, because normally a code clerk's movements were very circumscribed and his free time limited. It was an arrangement that suited the code clerk perfectly; being cooped up in that security-tight code room all day, doing that tedious work of enciphering messages or the routine of transmitting and receiving them might well have driven him a little stir-crazy. And he seemed to have a hyperactive libido. In some combination, this accounted for the frequency and regularity of his sexual escapades, which he must have known Soviet security would frown upon.

That vulnerability of the code clerk presented us with the makings of an operation. A code clerk is one of the highest priority targets, and means of access to them are so few and far between that we wanted this operation to be airtight. The key to the operation necessarily was the woman who would become the code clerk's steady paramour. It required a woman who would understand the role she was playing and who could play that role in the direction we wanted the operation to go. Finding the right person called for Eduardo's talents.

There was no dearth of prostitutes in Mexico City, from the crudest to the most sophisticated. But we were hesitant about picking a local person who might have a lot of explaining to do to friends in her set, or might not be able to resist the temptation to talk. So, willy nilly, we became white slavers. Eduardo thought he could find just the right person in Vera Cruz, which was almost a second home to him.

I had daily telephone contact with Eduardo in Vera Cruz in a perfectly secure manner, from a street booth, our conversation conducted in the kind of double talk that is second nature to intelligence operatives. Within a day or two, Eduardo had found the perfect person, attractive, smart, and free to come or go as she chose. By telephone I conveyed to

Eduardo the unfolding dimensions of the operation to guide him in the way he might approach her, the promises of money and other rewards he might make, the conditions she would be likely to meet in the operation once she was brought to Mexico City. And on successive days Eduardo would report his findings and render his judgment.

Our plan consisted of inserting "our" prostitute in the path of the code clerk's lusts. She would be installed in an apartment in the immediate vicinity of the Soviet Embassy. She would immediately play up to the ego of this lonely man, showing affection and a personal interest in his thoughts and his problems. Our plan could hardly go beyond that point, although there were several options dependent on the relationship between the two: We could record the conversations in the apartment, and if the Soviet had been indiscreet we could use the evidence to blackmail him; if necessary, we could rig up a camera to take photos of him in compromising situations; the woman, if she were the consummate actress we hoped to get, might lead the code clerk to forsake the Soviet fold; we could fake a "police" raid on the love nest; or some lucky break beyond our plotting might deliver our man.

We wished to keep the American hand from showing until the operation had reached the reaping stage. The burden to carry it along therefore fell on Eduardo's shoulders. He recruited the woman from Vera Cruz and returned to Mexico City to tell us all about her. He was enthusiastic, recounting her charms and the way she had caught on to the general outline of the scheme; she was satisfied with the money arrangement and delighted with the prospect of having her very own apartment. He busied himself in the tough assignment of locating a suitable apartment, with success in a relatively short time.

At about this stage of the operation I bowed out of active control and turned it over to another case officer of the station. But piecing together the bits that came my way, I believe that when Eduardo returned to Vera Cruz to pick up the prostitute and escort her back to Mexico City, she declined to participate any further. Eduardo then conducted a frantic search in Mexico City and came up with another candidate. I left Mexico shortly thereafter, and although I never learned how the operation finally came out, I was confident that in Eduardo the station had found the truly indispensable agent.

It is helpful to describe and explain the characteristics of a wide variety of agents in lesser roles that nevertheless are vital and necessary to the functioning of foreign intelligence. They are of two broad types, which may be called "developmental" and "action support."

Developmental Agents

Developmental agents, like most agents, are not discovered by case officers but present themselves to officials and thereby set themselves up for recruitment. They may be Americans or non-Americans, a distinction that has a bearing on their motivation for disclosing to United States authorities their association or contacts with Soviets or other communists. Non-Americans usually step forward because they do not wish to jeopardize their privileges, business or travel, with the U.S. Embassy. Americans most often do it from motives of sheer patriotism or fear of being tainted. Those who appear to the case officer to have potential for some operational use are recruited. As stringers with limited initial capacity for operational headway (hence the term "developmental") they usually are not paid for their services. But given their motivations, they generally prove to be enthusiastic and self-sacrificing once they are caught up in the spying game. I was personally associated while in Mexico with several types of developmental agents.

There was the non-American travel agent who had acquired a [fourteen words deleted]. The travel agent turned over to us all notices and requests for Soviet travel, including copies of the documents that are customarily required for international travel. Our interest, naturally, was to have advance notice, when possible, of the movement of Soviet personnel, as well as identifying data concerning them. It was a lazy kind of operation because all that was needed was for the agent to call in when he had something and for me to go pick it up. As far as we could tell from monitoring Soviet contacts with the travel agent, the KGB had no operational interest in him. So we were getting something out of it.

Another non-American, a Mexican, had formed a close social relationship with the top man in Soviet intelligence, a KGB Colonel whose apartment we bugged (more on this later). From the start we were suspicious of the Colonel's motive for prolonging the friendship, because our common Mexican friend was associated with [four words deleted] and was very knowledgeable of the [one word deleted] business. We tried to smoke out the Soviet's interest, and at the same time in a fairly low-key manner tried to maneuver our agent toward double agent status. Our agent, a very likeable and amiable fellow, either played dumb to our drift or wittingly and stubbornly resisted our efforts. We settled for the most advantageous exploitation we could get out of the social relationship with an important target. Once, we prevailed upon our agent to invite the Colonel and his family [seven words deleted] (with the idea of leaving the Colonel's apartment vacant), but took no operational advantage of the occasion. Generally, however, in accordance with recent Headquarters instructions to profile Soviet targets thoroughly, we used our amiable friend to report in detail on the personality and habits of the Colonel. He did that willingly enough, following my coaching on what to record, and by the time I left Mexico an ample dossier had been compiled on the Colonel. I never learned whether a subsequent approach had been made to the Colonel. This case had involved many meetings with the agent over a lengthy period, but with no more expenditure than lunches or dinners and drinks.

We also had on the string for a short period a young Mexican sports enthusiast whose major pastime was [one word deleted]. He was joined in that pastime by a young Soviet from the Soviet Embassy, who evidently was a [one word deleted] nut. The two became friendly to a point where the

Mexican became apprehensive and decided to tell American authorities about it. We told the young man that he had done the correct thing because his Soviet friend was indeed a junior intelligence officer of the KGB. We asked him to report to us complete details of his association with the Soviet, and particularly because of his friendship to try to worm out of the Soviet intimate aspects of his life in Mexico. Our agent tried valiantly, but unfortunately his reporting was abominable. He just was not a good observer, and he lacked the finesse to pry without seeming to do so. We agreed to drop the whole thing. A [one word deleted] court seemingly was not the arena for developing an operation, either on our part or on the Soviet's part.

With Americans as developmental agents you were playing in a different ballpark, because you had to assume that Soviets who maintained a relationship with Americans were probably cultivating them for a sinister purpose. Take the case of American students attending Mexico City College (later called University of the Americas). Soviet intelligence officers enrolled at the same university would strike up acquaintances with selected American students. The Soviets never came on strong at the start, but gradually deepened the relationship through casual intellectual discussion in the unworldly academic atmosphere of the school. The idealistic student, especially, was pretty much of a pushover for a trained intelligence officer. Acquaintanceship would progress to friendship; there were picnics, bar hopping, parties, by which time the Soviet would know whether he had the makings of a tool for his purposes.

The Soviets were not particularly interested in what American students could do for them in Mexico, but were following the classic espionage technique of developing and grooming potential assets who on return to their country might attain some status, especially in government. They went so far as to provide guidance and assistance to the students in applying for government jobs, in preparing for the Foreign Service examinations, etc. At the very least, for their effort, they may have succeeded in placing Soviets, the Soviet Union, or even communist doctrine in a more favorable and sympathetic light.

Some of these students, naturally (and Soviet intelligence officers would so anticipate), reported what was going on to American authorities in Mexico. Those students best suited for a double agent role we recruited, and the others we cautioned to break off their association with the Soviets. Consequently, Mexico City Station was preoccupied with a number of these student double agent operations. They involved an inordinate amount of case officer time: meeting, coaching, and training the student agents, and processing voluminous reports. At Headquarters these reports were read and indexed by the counterintelligence people — presumably to nail down the methods of operation of the KGB in this type of approach. Our student agents reported to us on contacts made by the Soviets with other students who did not reveal them to us. I cannot help thinking in hindsight that conversion of these operations to double agent operations may have been counterproductive. Any self-respecting KGB intelligence officer, innately suspicious that his pigeon may have been doubled back on him, would have little difficulty in detecting the awkward efforts of a fledgling conspirator to hurl himself or herself deeper into the embrace of the Soviets. With this edge, the Soviets could easily manage the operation to their advantage, by tying up case officer time and effort, winding us up in paperwork, and having us chase false leads all over the lot.

We had a somewhat puzzling operation that dragged on with a mature [one word deleted] woman who worked in the cartographic section of a [one word deleted]. She was visited regularly by a Soviet who purchased ordinary maps of the lands and waters of Latin America and brought her small gifts from time to time. We pegged the Soviet as a member of the GRU, the military component of the RIS. Certainly the requirement to collect maps was consistent with the interests of the GRU. It was also consistent with GRU operational technique to commence an operation of this type with normal demands for unclassified materials, to lull the suspicions of a prospective agent under cultivation. But this program of making innocuous purchases and plying the woman with gifts went on for years. We played along, growing a little more desperate as time went on to stage scenarios with our agent that she could play with the Soviet to convince him that she was ripe for recruitment. She dutifully tried at each subsequent visit from the intelligence officer, but he never took the hint. She was still trying when I left Mexico.

Several American businessmen of [one word deleted] firms crossed the paths of Soviet intelligence officers, usually of the GRU. The pattern initiated by the Soviet was pretty standard. The Soviet intelligence officers used in these operations were personable, mature, educated types who could mix more readily than most Soviets with educated American businessmen. After rapport had been established, the Soviets would cement the relationship by [five words deleted]. The Soviet and the American would invariably enter into discussions of the field of the American's scientific expertise, and it was not just a one-way street, since the Soviet would contribute helpful knowledge to the American. Later along in the operation, the Soviet would begin to probe for specific information he was seeking. Depending on the stage of this pattern at which we entered the situation, we could coach our American agent along until the moment of truth arrived. When we knew what it was the GRU was after, it was time to terminate the operation. We had our American agent ease out by dodging questions on the taboo subject and letting lapse the social ties. As case officer for the American businessmen I can attest that they were fine actors; only the scientific analysts back at Headquarters would know if there had been any worthwhile information developed from the operation.

The last of the developmental agents that stand out in my memory was a woman [one word deleted] about thirty years of age. She, like a surprising number of [two words deleted], was "trying out" Mexico as a way of life. She had become part of the arty crowd of Mexicans and Americans and other foreigners who hung around the cafes and art shops of the tourist section. As best I could gather, she formed fitful liaisons with men to supplement a rather small income she had from [two words deleted]. She was, however, goodlooking, jolly, and had an enormous bust. I don't know which of her qualities it was that attracted the attention, at a soiree given at the Soviet Embassy, of an unmarried handsome Soviet, an intelligence officer.

Although our potential Mata Hari met the Soviet on other occasions, it was always in mixed company and our agent was candid enough to say that the Soviet wasn't exactly panting after her. With our agent quite resigned to sacrifice her honor for the good of [two words deleted], we tried by various ruses to foster romance, but they all fell through. When I left Mexico, our agent was still on the "available" list.

Action Support Agents

I have just a few examples of the other type of agent with an action support role. Though minor, the problem of recruiting this type of agent was both tricky and risky. We learned of two, at different times, through monitoring the [two words deleted] to the Soviet Embassy. In one case, the Soviets would call upon the same supplier to deliver [one word deleted] to the Embassy. The [two words deleted], just an ordinary Mexican scratching to make a living, was puzzled by our interest but succumbed to our blandishment of money to go along and report to us on physical features inside the Soviet Embassy. Through debriefing the man, we became excited when he described one delivery point which we believed could well be the communications room of the embassy. What we didn't tell him was that at some time in the future he might be asked to secrete some object somewhere in the embassy.

The other agent was a one-shot deal that involved the agent's firm, which was to supply and install some kind of wiring in the embassy. This was a push hard operation with the agent, who was reluctant to undertake it, and, in fact, nothing came of it.

There was a third lead that came from the same source as the other two. We learned that a cabinet-maker with a small shop was given the order by the Soviets to make and install shelving in the embassy. I went to the shop to case the situation. It was not like walking into a grocery store, buying some soda pop, and striking up a conversation. I had to have a legitimate reason for gaining entry to the cabinet-maker's shop, which called for a little investment by the station. I made a sketch of a small piece of furniture I wanted and walked into the shop. The owner said sure, he could make it for about 400 pesos. I left the sketch with the promise that the piece would be ready in about two weeks. That didn't bother me, because I would become the anxious purchaser and come around often before the two weeks were up. I did, but every time I came I saw only the owner's helper to whom my job had been turned over. Finally, after two weeks, I called and picked up the finished article. The owner was there. Where had he been all those times I had come in previously? Oh, he said, he had been busy installing shelves in the Soviet Embassy. Bert consoled me by saying he might be able to use that weird little wooden stand I had designed, somewhere in the office.

18

EXTRACURRICULAR OPERATIONS:
Political Actions and Case Officer as Agent

SOME operations in Mexico were a far cry from my daily rounds. I have noted that I had little to do with paramilitary or political action, which in the main was directed and coordinated by a Headquarters covert action staff. At Mexico City Station, however, which was one of the largest and best operated of the Clandestine Services' stations, there was a highly rated covert action case officer. In the course of his duties he dreamed up a political action operation which required the specific use of one of my agents. That is how I became involved in political action.

Agent of Political Action

The operation was targeted against a prominent Latin American statesman (liberal in the Latin sense) then in political asylum in Mexico City but planning to return to his country to run for president. The idea behind the operation was to give public evidence of his countrymen's opposition to the statesman's return, and possibly to discourage him or frighten him from his intentions. The plan was simple: A small pencil-size bomb (with little shatter but much clatter) was to be placed outside the door to the statesman's apartment. When it went off and brought a police investigation, the covert action officer would see to it, through his press outlets, that the incident received the proper interpretation.

As luck would have it, I had an agent, whom I shall call

Sergio, who was living in the same apartment building as the statesman. The mechanics of the operation were therefore turned over to me. Sergio joined the plot enthusiastically, even though he understood that he was tagged to place the bomb.

The operation was set for about one a.m., when the statesman and his family should have been sound asleep. Even though Sergio had been thoroughly briefed by one of our technicians on the properties and timing characteristics of the pencil bomb, it was not to be turned over to him until shortly before it was set to go off. That complicated the preparations immensely. Sergio's building had an all-night guard who was stationed at the front door. It was planned, therefore, that Sergio would drive his car into the garage (first-floor level) very late that night, and leave the side door to the garage open. Then at the proper time Sergio would descend the stairway from his apartment and enter the garage, which could be done without being seen from the front door area. We would have someone with the primed pencil bomb stationed close to the side door who would pass it over to Sergio as soon as he appeared. Sergio then would reascend to his apartment via the stairs, stopping en route to place the bomb at the statesman's door. All the usual security precautions, including lookouts to spot anything unusual, were set.

We really earned our title as "spooks" that misty moonlit night, as all participants glided into place. All eyes were glued to the side door. Right on schedule, the door opened silently. The technician, guardian of the pencil bomb up to the last, walked swiftly to the door, remained there a few seconds, and faded away into the shadows. We all remained in the vicinity for five minutes or so, until we were certain that Sergio had carried out his mission without mishap, and then scattered to our homes.

I called the station as soon as the working day had begun to find out what had been heard of the blast. They had no word. I called Sergio at work, detected only chagrin in his voice, and arranged to meet him within the hour. When we met, he shook his head and expressed puzzlement. He said he had placed the bomb on the hallway floor just outside the statesman's door. He stayed awake the half hour or so until the time it was set to go off. He waited longer, thinking that the timing may have been off. He wanted to take a look, but decided it was too risky. Earlier than usual, he set off for work and deliberately passed by the door of the statesman. The pencil bomb had disappeared. He noted that the hallways had already been swept. He swore by his favorite saint that everything he told me was absolutely true, exactly as it had happened.

We case officers could do no better in our postmortems. Perhaps the statesman had discovered the bomb in the dead of night; he was very politically savvy and would have known what to do with it. If that were so, it was not likely that he would have reported it to the police or given notoriety to the incident in any way. Or perhaps the janitor while sweeping the dimly lit halls might have caught the pencil-size object up with the rest of the trash. But if some knowledgeable person had not dismantled it in time, why had the bomb not exploded? Was it a dud? The technician explained that this type of bomb was usually reliable, but it was possible that the timing mechanism or detonator could have failed. (I think there was a liquid chemical that through chemical reaction of a known elapsed time set the bomb off.) Or, there was the possibility that Sergio had lost his nerve and was lying; or that Sergio for reasons of his own had decided not to go through with the operation and had disposed of the bomb in some other way. I, who knew Sergio best, stoutly defended him and stated unequivocally that he had told the truth.

Yet fully a month later I was informed that a polygraph operator was coming to Mexico City and I was to set Sergio up for a test session without telling him its specific purpose. That wasn't easy; I gave him the usual line that all our agents are periodically subjected to lie detector examinations, that it was good security and so forth, but both Sergio and I knew the real reason for the followup. I brought Sergio to the hotel room where the apparatus had been set up. I waited outside while he underwent the examination. When Sergio emerged he looked somber and shaken; as I conducted him out of the hotel he confirmed that the operator had asked questions concerning the bomb incident. I told him not to worry as I left him. Then I doubled back into the hotel and up to the operator's room. The operator was looking over the tracings. To my unspoken question, he said that Sergio had come through fine. Though relieved that the verdict favored Sergio, I retained my skepticism of a machine and its human operator that were equally as capable of truth rejection as of lie detection.

The pencil bomb operation remained a mystery. In my estimation, it was just as well that it failed. Unlike espionage and counterintelligence operations, or even propaganda operations, action operations of a political or paramilitary nature do not have the game quality to which the former have been reduced. The latter have consequences that go beyond a mere adversary relationship, consequences that are unforeseen, uncontrolled, and unmindful of the harm and privation caused to others. The results of such operations prove to be useless at best and counterproductive at worst when aimed at political or military situations far removed from the American understanding. The paramilitary intervention in Laos and the political action support to the ouster of Allende in Chile are cases in point.

Case Officer as Agent

There are circumstances, as I discovered in Cuba, when a case officer without agents must perform as an agent himself. There was no lack of agents in Mexico, however, and on those occasions that I acted as an agent it was because a regular agent wouldn't do.

One small job involved a local dentist who was taking care of the dental needs of the Soviet Embassy, including the teeth of a few fellows we were interested in. In its encompassing pursuit of minutiae about Soviets, the station thought it was worth a whirl to extract from the dentist any tidbits of information he might drop under skillful questioning. I was picked for this assignment not long after I had arrived in Mexico, and fortuitously as a tartar-builder of note I had a set of teeth that needed cleaning. I planned that during the first visit as soon as the dentist started to examine my teeth for cavities, I would strive to establish conversational rapport with him leading to the subject of his "foreign" clientele. I vaguely felt that a second visit might be required to pursue the matter of the dentist's Soviet patients further, but optimistically left that to chance. If I were lucky, I might have a cavity to be filled, or might go for broke on those missing back teeth. After all, it wasn't going to cost me a cent.

As affably as possible I settled into the dentist's chair and awaited the examination. As the dentist perfunctorily tapped and probed inside my mouth I tried to release some conversational gems, but received only annoyed looks in return. During the cleaning, which lasted about fifteen minutes, I was unable to get out a complete sentence. While he was leading me to the office to pay the bill, I asked desperately if he had any other foreign patients. He replied, "Yes, all kinds," took my money, and waved me out. When I reported to Bert the results of my visit, he said not to give the matter a second thought and promptly made out a voucher to reimburse me for the money I had laid out. Later, out of a lingering sense of failure, I made an appointment for my wife with the same dentist and accompanied her, hoping for that chance of a followup of the original mission. Nothing happened; that bill was paid for out of pocket.

I was chosen for a similar mission, this time with a doctor who was treating Soviet patients, for probably the same reason: no official link to the United States Embassy. But the guidelines for approach to the doctor were different: I could represent myself as affiliated with the United States government and I would make a cold pitch for the doctor's cooperation. When I was closeted with the doctor, I glibly insinuated my intelligence role on behalf of the U.S. government and its support of the Mexican government, and said that we were aware of the fact the doctor had Soviet patients under his care. The doctor said nothing. I hastened to explain that we were not interested in medical information about his patients, but only in other personal information that the doctor might glean during their visits or if he should be summoned to the Soviet Embassy. The doctor seemed to ponder my remarks, but then quietly responded that he could do nothing that violated the doctor-patient relationship. It might have been unprofessional, but frankly I was relieved. Face to face with my quarry, it became apparent to me that what we were after (what *were* we after?) wasn't worth the candle. I thanked the doctor for allowing us the opportunity to talk to him, and bowed out of that mission by telling the doctor that we understood and approved his unwillingness to divulge privileged information.

One case in which I played agent involved chasing after, stalking, and capturing an American spy. At least, the latter is what I set out to do. In the United States, the FBI had uncovered a Soviet spy case that involved an American Army sergeant who had skipped. There was a report that the sergeant had gone to Tampico, Mexico. I was sent to find him.

When I arrived in Tampico, a major shipping port on the east coast of Mexico, I checked in with the U.S. consul, who had been advised of my coming. I had photographs of the sergeant; the consul said he had heard nothing unusual about any American in Tampico the last few days. I then briefed the consul on my cover while in Tampico, the hotel I would be staying at, a communications system I would use with him, and my general plans for possibly spotting the sergeant. We worked out a scheme for utilizing the Mexican police to effect the capture.

The plan? Easy. Put yourself in the shoes of a military man on the loose in a seaport town. The focal point of the search would naturally be the red-light district, the brothels, the sleazy bars, and the late-hour eating joints by night; by day, the busy intersections of the shopping district. Plans are easy to spin out. Putting them into practice is another matter. A different way of saying it, but striking just as hard at the major flaw in intelligence work, is the failure to recognize the vast distinction between intentions and feasibility.

At night, dressed in the sloppiest clothes I had, I slouched through the streets of the disreputable part of town. Somehow among all those other slouching men I was attracting considerable attention from the ladies of the evening. The answer was obvious: They spotted me for an *Americano* from way off. They emerged from darkened doorways, sidled up to me, and bluntly asked if I would partake of their charms, some using what they considered to be enticing American slang. Invariably I quickened my pace and fended them off in Spanish, even though my plan had been to question some about other *Americanos* they had run into recently.

I never realized how tiring it could be just to walk through a red-light district. At one point I ducked into what appeared to be a small, better class restaurant and sat down at a table. A moment later, a woman entered, walked over to my table, and sat down. She was a mature woman, not a young thing; her mascara and eye shadow couldn't hide the tired lines in her face, and her body had long ago lost its trimness. Sitting sideways to me, she hunched her dress over her knees, leaned toward me exposing her bosom, and asked me to order a beer for her. I did, and an orange drink and cheese sandwich for myself. We talked for half an hour. I declined her invitation to go to her rooms, and she gave up telling me how happy she could make me. She then began to speak of her hard lot in life — no husband, several kids, no work, so she had become a streetwalker, and what a distasteful and unrewarding life it was. I told her I was looking for an American friend, and I gave a physical description of the sergeant. She hadn't seen an *Americano* like that, but maybe some of her friends had. I gave her twenty pesos, saying I might be around the neighborhood the next night, and I left.

Meanwhile, back at the ranch-like motel where I was staying, I ran into cover trouble. There were a few Americans around who descended on me like a long lost relative. I told them I was a writer who had come to Tampico for some local color. For some inexplicable reason, they concluded that I was Carter Brown, a well known writer of paperbacks, using a pseudonym. The more I demurred, the firmer they were in their belief. When I took my final leave of them, they shouted their good-byes to the famous author they really thought I was.

I remained two nights and two days in Tampico. I put in two long vigils on the streets of the busiest part of town, scanning the faces of any likely passersby, munching nourishment at open food stands. I went back to the red-light district the second night, did not encounter my companion of the night before, and dropped into a few bars, where it seemed decidedly unhealthy for an American to be. Worn and tired, I reported to the consul that our man was nowhere to be seen. I took the evening plane back to Mexico City.

Later, when the sergeant was finally taken into custody by the FBI, it was discovered that he had never been in Tampico.

19

HIGH-TECH SURVEILLANCE:
The KGB Colonel

PERHAPS the most grandiose operation that fell to my stewardship while I was in Mexico had as its target none other than the *Rezident* of the Soviet KGB in Mexico.

Operation Summit

The stars seemed to have fallen into place for this one. The highest-ranking Soviet intelligence officer in the country, a Colonel of the KGB, whose powers and mandate might easily exceed those of the Soviet Ambassador, had presumably decided to live it up a little. He moved to one of the finer, expensive apartment buildings [six words deleted]. There he lived with his family, apart from the usual security barriers that surround one in his position. Thus in theory at least he became fair game as a prospective target. But there was a hitch. The high-rise building in which he lived had no other tall buildings in the vicinity close enough to serve as a listening post in the event that the Colonel's apartment could be successfully bugged, and there were no vacancies in his apartment building.

But all that changed suddenly one day when a "Vacancy" sign appeared in a window. It signaled the beginning of Operation Summit, with a rush. We had to get that vacant apartment; we had to get an agent to occupy it — not any old agent, but one who could fit in with the luxury surroundings — and we had to do it fast. One of our most trusted agents saved the day; he recommended a personal friend, the same Sergio of the pencil-bomb operation. By the next day, Sergio had a signed lease for the apartment in his hand. He was to be paid all expenses of moving, breaking the lease where he was living, and a monthly salary that covered the stiff rental of the new apartment and then some.

Sergio's apartment was [five words deleted], but not directly beneath. But it was advantageously placed to afford ample opportunity for the kind of internal surveillance of the Colonel and his family that was required. And so, with Sergio's participation we started the same kind of detailed observation utilized in Operation Surprise. Sergio's wife was cut in, too.

The station, using its formidable array of photographic coverage, taps, and physical surveillance, dogged the footsteps of the Colonel until we were able to predict where he would be before he even thought about it himself. The pattern revealed the one thing we were looking for: an extended period of time when it might be fairly certain that the Colonel and his family would be absent from the apartment. The Colonel, evidently a good family man as well as a devotee of good living, had been regularly visiting his wife and children at the Soviet Embassy's summer retreat in Cuernavaca over the weekend. We had sufficient time to plan and carry out the entry to the Colonel's apartment.

On the weekend selected, with an airtight system of security precautions in place, we were ready to go. Some of the gear that the technicians required had already been brought to Sergio's apartment. The technicians brought the remainder and based themselves in his apartment. With Sergio acting as lookout, the technicians scooted up to the Colonel's apartment and were inside in a matter of seconds. In about an hour they had completed their work, placing one bug in the living room close to the sofa and another in the bedroom. They retreated to Sergio's apartment and tested the microphones through the receiving and recording equipment that would be left in the listening post, Sergio's own bedroom. Shortly thereafter they left, the mikes working perfectly, and rejoined Bert and me, where we celebrated and went over the whole episode.

I was in charge of the operation, although there were some aspects in which I would not be personally involved. For instance, a small team of translators was on hand in Mexico City and would receive the reels of tapes of recorded conversations that Sergio would turn over periodically to one of the translators. The translations were scanned in the station for significant information and for any indications that the installation might have become compromised, or known to the Soviets. Copies were sent to Headquarters, where they were reviewed and studied for counterintelligence material of value or positive intelligence. This operation was unquestionably on the big time list of home buggings of RIS personnel toward which the Clandestine Services had recently turned attention and emphasis.

This was a long-time working operation; it would be fully a year before the batteries of the transmitters ran out. It is difficult to calculate its cost, in case officer time, agent time, translator time, in equipment and materials used, in reels of tape, in agent salary, in cost of renting the apartment, in Headquarters handling and analyst review time, in paper consumed, etc. But it must easily have hit six figures. No doubt about it, it was "big time" and a model of technical operational competence.

What was the grade, value, or level of the intelligence we collected? I blush to put the question now, because at the time it hadn't occurred to me to raise it. I can best describe the results as "Three Hundred Sixty-five Days in the (Home) Life of Ivan Denisovich." We had an exact tally on the love life of the Colonel, toilet-training technique Soviet style, shopping lists and supermarket prices, husband-wife spats, and all the trivia of folksy apartment living. When the Colonel and his wife had visitors, there were reams of small talk to plough through.

But the secrets of running the KGB intelligence effort in Mexico remained locked up in the head of the Colonel. The Colonel evidently preferred to have meetings with his secret agents elsewhere than in his home. If he had discovered that he was bugged, he even disdained to double the bug back on us by cleverly feeding misleading information to us.

Judging by the barren yield of the harvest, the operation was a complete bust. It pays to examine why, since such results are usual for the majority of operations directed against well-established adversaries. In the Colonel's case, it was the height of folly to expect that a senior officer of the KGB would violate security by blabbing intelligence secrets to his wife or anyone else in the unguarded confines of his home. Or to think that he would have secret agents come to his home. Or that he would discuss "his" business even with colleagues from the Soviet Embassy who might be visiting. Had we looked coldly at these factors, and beyond the fervor to fashion and construct a technically superior operation, we probably would never have gone ahead with it, even if the stars seemed to have fallen into place.

At the heart of this exercise in electronic eavesdropping is a single salient factor to which little or no attention is paid. Abroad, at any rate, the adversary *knows* he is the adversary. That conviction, that he is an enemy, has been dinned into him over a long period of time. The RIS abroad, the intelligence services of the communist countries, the official representatives of communist countries, the local Communist Party, leftist groups, radical students, and anti-government factions are the primary targets of the action arm of the CIA, the Clandestine Services. For survival's sake, these target entities have become very security conscious and wary of airing their secrets except under the most secure conditions. In the United States the same relationship prevails. Those criminal elements that violate federal laws *know* they are the enemy of the FBI and practice their security accordingly. The chiefs or members of the Mafia are not likely to transact their nefarious business over open phones nor to plot their nefarious schemes in other than thoroughly safe surroundings. At the very least, the practitioners of electronic eavesdropping, wiretaps, or bugging should exercise a little cost-consciousness (for the taxpayers' sake) before heaving like an elephant to produce a mouse.

I should note that the reverse of the above law also holds true. If the "adversary" does not expect or know that he is the adversary, or that he is on the "enemies list," then he exhibits little or no caution in his telephone or conversational habits. But by the same token, such an adversary, who is innocent of crime and is not plotting or carrying out illegal acts, will inevitably disappoint his eager listeners. The orders of the White House to tap the phones of suspects who might be leaks for national security material were incredibly naive: Those who *were* furnishing leaks to some outside party would not advertise the breach over phones assigned to their name; those who were *not* might well confide scraps of intimate detail to their phones, but little else, and certainly not a word on the subject for which they were being tapped. The paranoia for electronic eavesdropping obscures common sense to the point that proportion and reality fade out of the picture.

20

Conclusions

AFTER five years in Mexico as an operational officer under deep cover, I returned to the United States and to a desk job at Headquarters, where even though the work was absorbing, life was more sedate.

There was, however, one last electronic surveillance operation I handled at Headquarters that seemed to sum up much of my experience with the CIA and re-enforce my conclusions about many of its activities. If the operation against the Colonel was shooting high, this one was shooting for the moon, and landing. A bug had been placed in the office of a Soviet ambassador. A team of translators was kept busy overtime just trying to keep pace with the outpouring of conversations from that office. I had to read the entire "take" and cull from it the significant items. One result was undeniable: We had what amounted to a visitors' list to the ambassador, and even better, identifications of the speakers (an expertise the transcribers acquire). Tuned in, as it were, to a motherlode of information, we should have been gathering handfuls of nuggets. Sad to say, there were no nuggets. What I read page after page after page were the bumbling efforts of a fairly decent guy, the ambassador, to manage the politics-strewn affairs of a bureaucracy, the embassy. When an occasional streak of yellow showed, due to interest in a particular visitor, it turned out to be fool's gold. Rendering Russian, or any foreign language for that matter, into English plays tricks with meaning; the tape doesn't pick up hand or body movements, or facial expressions, or any of the physical accompaniments to speech that often convey the essence of dialogue.

This operation would have been worth the colossal outlay of time and money, but not to us. An Inspector General of the U.S.S.R. Ministry of Foreign Affairs would have drooled to have this inside picture of how one of the embassies under his jurisdiction was being run. The Clandestine Services is simply not interested in that kind of information, and the greater irony was that even if they wanted to pass such information on to others, so super-secret and sensitive was the operation that reporting tended to be repressed for fear of compromising or disclosing the source.

This final operation only confirmed my deeply held conviction that intelligence agencies delude themselves if they believe that the fruits of intelligence collection lead to divining the "intentions" of the enemy or anyone else. Like trying to divine the prospective effect of propaganda on an uncontrolled audience, it is empirically impossible to leap into the minds of individuals, friend or foe. Yet the leap is made with assurance and little hesitation by the intelligence community, particularly in their own specialties. Let it be discovered, for instance, that the Soviets have considerably upped the stockpiling of meat, and the analysts rush into print with "early warning" of an impending Soviet hostile move. The Defense Intelligence Agency is stubbornly psychic in discerning emplacements, disposition, and technological advances in weapons, or movements and maneuvers of troops, as indications of hostile tactics or strategy. It seldom occurs to those hitched to a fixed ideological star that the actions a country takes are generally consistent with its own rationally perceived needs or interests for its *own* survival or improvement. The capacity for self-delusion is not limited to American intelligence agencies. Our Soviet friends are prone to the same phenomenon, to the extent that they permit ideological blinders to distort their appreciation of reality.

Reality is distorted also in the conventional view of the foreign activities of the KGB and GRU as ruthless, an impression fostered even by the late Allen W. Dulles, former Director of the CIA, in his book *The Craft of Intelligence*. The fact is that the KGB, the Committee of State Security, displays ruthlessness towards its *own* nationals who are considered traitors to the motherland (emigres, defectors, and the like). The harrowing exploits of the KGB's "Executive Action" branch, the long string of kidnappings and assassinations, make for very sober reading; but KGB behavior towards nationals of other countries is no different from that of other intelligence services. Judging from the vantage point of double agent operations, I believe Soviet professional behavior is as harmless as ours.

The duel between the rival intelligence services, the CIA and the KGB, has been universally depicted as deadly, daggers bared, and no holds barred — an image perpetuated by a generation of fiction writers. That view, by my opinion formed through twenty-seven years as an intelligence officer of the National Security Agency and the CIA, is a fallacy. The truth is that, apart from covert operations, the jousting between the professionals of both services is benign and no one on either side (with the possible exception of hapless agents) gets hurt. The intrigue involved, the moves and countermoves, resemble nothing so much as an interminable chess game with no winners.

Ironically, in the classic duel of espionage and counter-intelligence between the services, the fiercely contending ideologies act as a drag-weight on clandestine performance. Clandestine warriors rush to engage in sterile operations for operations' sake. And, though driven by ideological animosities, the intelligence officers of both services seldom get bloodied, few are discomfited, and all seem to enjoy their role and the perquisites that go along with it.

But the twisted mythology of deadly warfare between the services, spawned by the atmospherics of Cold War and the clash of opposing ideologies, has had serious and profound political consequences. It has fed and heightened suspicions between the United States and the Soviet Union, and has entered the propaganda of both nations to inspire fear in their own populaces. It has diverted attention from the sobering truth that it is governments, not intelligence services, that initiate covert political and paramilitary actions. And by tarring classic intelligence rivalry with the same brush as politically inspired actions, it has obscured the fact that the latter (directed at third countries) raise moral and humanitarian questions that tarnish the quest toward universal peace, freedom, and stability.

Index

153

Index compiled by Daniel Tsang

Typesetting by

New Mississippi, Inc.
P. O. Box 3568
Jackson, MS 39207